1

LET'S MAKE
WHOOPIES!

LET'S MAKE WHOOPIES!

MEET THE NEW CUPCAKE ON THE BLOCK

SOPHIE GREY

PHOTOGRAPHY BY ALISTAIR RICHARDSON

MICHAEL JOSEPH
an imprint of
Penguin Books

TO MY PARENTS

MICHAEL JOSEPH

Published by the Penguin Group

Penguin Books Ltd, 80 Strand, London WC2R 0RL, England

Penguin Group (USA) Inc., 375 Hudson Street, New York, New York 10014, USA

Penguin Group (Canada), 90 Eglinton Avenue East, Suite 700, Toronto, Ontario, Canada M4P 2YR
(a division of Pearson Penguin Canada Inc.)

Penguin Ireland, 25 St Stephen's Green, Dublin 2, Ireland (a division of Penguin Books Ltd)

Penguin Group (Australia), 250 Camberwell Road, Camberwell, Victoria 3124, Australia
(a division of Pearson Australia Group Pty Ltd)

Penguin Books India Pvt Ltd, 11 Community Centre, Panchsheel Park, New Delhi – 110 017, India

Penguin Group (NZ), 67 Apollo Drive, Rosedale, Auckland 0632, New Zealand
(a division of Pearson New Zealand Ltd)

Penguin Books (South Africa) (Pty) Ltd, 24 Sturdee Avenue, Rosebank, Johannesburg 2196, South Africa

Penguin Books Ltd, Registered Offices: 80 Strand, London WC2R 0RL England

www.penguin.com

First published 2011
1

Copyright © Sophie Grey, 2011

Photography copyright © Alistair Richardson, 2011

Set in Helvetica Neue, Roice and Sackers Gothic

Printed and bound by Firmengruppe APPL, aprinta druck, Wemding, Germany

A CIP catalogue record for this book is available from the British Library

978–0–241–95348–8

www.greenpenguin.co.uk

Penguin Books is committed to a sustainable
future for our business, our readers and our
planet. This book is made from paper certified
by the Forest Stewardship Council.

CONTENTS

INTRODUCTION

My first forays into baking involved following a *Blue Peter* recipe when I was six years old. The recipe was for chocolate muffins with a teaspoon of vinegar! The mixture spent much of the time on the floor, consisted of far too much vinegar and looked revolting, but – of course – my dad ate them and said they were delicious. At university I studied physiology and pharmacology – I think that's where my love of mixing and recipe testing came from. While my peers were in the student bar I was giving large dinner parties at home. After university I continued to give dinner parties, and one day my friend Jackie suggested I should cater for a friend of hers, Simon, who was throwing a party for 100 people in Chelsea Harbour. The Simon was Simon Cowell.

He wanted something simple and traditional, so I got out my Delia Smith *Complete Cookery Course* and multiplied by twenty-five. I cooked a ratatouille and meat lasagne, three salads, a squidgy chocolate log and a tiramisù. It was a huge success and I really enjoyed it, so I thought a catering business would be fun. Since I was modelling at the time, I decided to use models to serve the food and called the company Model Catering – delicious food served by gorgeous girls. The business is still running today – we cater for film premières, private parties and weddings, and still occasionally cook for Simon.

When the recession hit a few years ago, I started to wonder what sort of food people might want to spend their money on as a treat to cheer themselves up, and came up with the idea of really good bread and cakes – indulgent comfort food. I started testing my recipes at home, and, much to his delight, every day my husband, Harry, would come home to a freshly baked loaf or cake. I've always been ambitious, and found myself getting a little bored of making just one or two items, so one evening he walked into the house to find the kitchen covered in flour – it was baking (pardon the pun) hot, since the oven had been on all day, and there were three bread crates on the table full of ciabatta and cakes. He looked at everything, then at me, and simply said, 'It's the crazy baker!' The name stuck, and I decided to call my business the Crazy Baker.

My friend Richard Bertinet is a fantastic master baker (and is the author of books called *Dough*, *Crust* and *Cook*). After my mad stint of baking different loaves and cakes at home, he came to London for the weekend early in 2009 and tried my bread. He immediately suggested I take it to some delis for them to try out, so I did. As a result, my first customer was Betty Blythe in Brook Green, reputedly the best establishment in London in which to eat cake. In March that year the business expanded and started delivering to shops and pubs, as well as delis, throughout the west London area. I'm pleased to say that I now have plenty of customers, both north and south of the river. The business operates twenty-four hours a day and I love the craziness of it all. The icing on the cake (!) was when we won the 2009 National Cupcake Competition with our Crazy Lemon Drizzle Cupcake (see page 112).

When a close friend of mine, Rebecca, moved to New York last summer, I asked her what the bakeries in Manhattan were making and she immediately said, 'Whoopie pies.' I did a little research and found that these are made from sandwiching together two partially risen sponges with a filling, sometimes capped with a set topping. I tried making some and thought they were fabulous. It then occurred to me that the set toppings could be used to accentuate a theme and could also be flavoured to complement or contrast with the filling and sponge. What's more, you could pick a whoopie up in one hand and eat it without getting frosting all over your face – perfect for parties. My mind started racing with all the possibilities!

I decided to start offering whoopies to clients and kicked off by making the classic chocolate whoopie on page 45. When an ad agency asked me to make 600 cupcakes for them for Valentine's Day, I suggested they have whoopies instead. So I set about making 10cm wide whoopies (for sharing) with a basic chocolate sponge and a delicious tangy cream cheese filling, topped with bright red or pink icing and sprinkles. Presented in individual boxes with tissue paper surrounds, they were a complete hit. (You can find smaller versions of this Valentine's whoopie on page 192.)

So where does the whoopie originate? Well, it is thought that Amish women in Pennsylvania baked the first whoopie pies for putting in their husbands' lunch boxes. After a hard morning's work the men opened them at lunchtime and shouted 'Whoopie!' As indeed my husband does now when we send samples down to his office!

With lots of ideas in my head for developing our range of whoopies, I came up with a whole collection of classical flavours, from vanilla to red velvet, gingerbread to lemon meringue, and a never-ending list of chocolate-based ones. I began to create whoopies for different types of celebration – from birthdays to Easter and Mother's and Father's Day. Next came a range for people with allergies. Then all kinds of different wacky whoopies in the shape of animals, which are perfect for children's parties. And since this all started with the fact that I was a caterer, I decided to create a selection of beautifully flavoured savoury whoopies which are based on canapés. They all taste delightful.

Having this plethora of whoopie ideas, I thought it would be a good idea to share some of them with you – so here is the *Let's Make Whoopies!* cookbook. Here you will find over seventy whoopie recipes and over thirty cupcakes, all from the kitchens of the Crazy Baker. All simple and easy to follow, they have been tested and can be made in a domestic kitchen, using everyday utensils and equipment. Even my little boys have had a go at helping to make some of them, and their whoopies came out perfectly edible. I hope you will have as much fun creating, baking and enjoying these creations as I have. Whoopie!

Sophie

TIPS, EQUIPMENT AND INGREDIENTS

+ BAKING TIPS

Size of whoopies

Please be aware that because of the vagaries of different ovens and the likelihood of your dollop of mixture being slightly bigger or smaller than the sizes I've stated in the recipes, your whoopies may turn out to be slightly bigger or smaller than mine. As long as they taste good, don't worry.

Larger cakes

As well as making brilliant whoopies, each of the recipes in the book can be made into a large cake too. Just pop the mixture into 2 prepared 20cm baking tins and bake at 180°C/350°F/gas 4 for about 25 minutes.

Ovens

All ovens are different, so get to know how yours works. I have tried the recipes using three different ovens – once you try a recipe in your own oven you will see how it bakes for you. The heat gives the whoopie sponge the rise it needs, but the sponges need to be baked through, and this means the temperature can't be too high, as this will result in burnt edges and a raw middle. If you take the sponges out too soon, the whoopies will drop, so if this happens cook your next batch a little longer. If your oven isn't big enough to take a whole batch, just bake in smaller batches as they will hold well for 15–20 minutes.

Temperature

The whoopies are baked at 200°C, whereas the cupcakes are baked at around 180°C. I've found that these are the best temperatures in the ovens I've tried them in. If you find that your whoopies are a bit crunchy at this temperature, reduce it by 10°, and if they are too soft, bake them for a minute longer

Storage

All these whoopie and cupcake sponges keep really well, covered, for 2–3 days. The chocolate sponges last even longer. All the sponges can be frozen.

Advance preparation

The icings and fillings can be made the day before, which is good if you are busy. On the day you need your whoopies or cupcakes, all you need to do is start decorating them without any pressure and really enjoy your creativity.

Cupcake cases

We use large muffin cases for our cupcakes and generally make 12 out of a batch of mixture. In our muffin cases the sponge rises to a few millimetres below the top. Most standard muffin cases from the supermarkets make 12 cupcakes that rise to the top. If you need them just below the surface, as you do for the wacky cupcakes, especially if you are topping them with water icing, make 13 – a baker's dozen. (Bakers in Henry III's reign were severely punished if they short-changed their customers, so rather than having their hand chopped off they would sell 13 items for the price of 12 –good idea!) It also helps to make an extra cupcake, just in case – for example if one is slightly burnt, or you drop one, or you would just like to test one before giving them to your guests. 'Just in case' is a bit of a motto of mine. I have said it most days for the last twenty years.

Supermarket fairy cake cases make 21 cupcakes out of a batch of mixture. Canapé cases make 96 out of a batch (halve the recipe if you don't want this many).

Lemon and lime curd

This can be made by an all-in-one method, as described in the recipes. Place all the ingredients in a saucepan over a medium heat and stir continuously and vigorously. The ingredients will melt and thicken. This should take 8 minutes, but you have to be vigilant.

Wacky/celebration whoopies and cupcakes

Make the sponges the day before and keep them covered until you need them. They will be easier to work with if they are slightly firmer. Piping may look frightening, but it's not that difficult. Once your whoopies or cupcakes are finished, I promise you they will look amazing.

To fill a piping bag

Place a measuring jug on your work surface. Place the piping bag in the jug and fold the top over the edges of the jug so you have an open hole. Fill the bag.

Special whoopie tip

When piping or dolloping whoopie mix on to baking trays, space well apart to prevent them spreading into one another.

Special cupcake tips

If a dome appears on your cupcakes the temperature of your oven is too high, so drop it down by 10°C.

To make it easier to work

+ Keep everything clean as you go. If your work surface is clean your mind is clear. It is very difficult to bake when you are stressed.

+ Get all the ingredients ready before you start. Place empty bowls in the sink as you go along, so you always have a clean work surface. Once your mixture is in the oven, wash up and clean your work surface before you move to the next stage.

+ You will create a nice flow of making, cleaning, making, cleaning . . . And you won't have a big mess at the end, just some lovely cakes to eat.

+ EQUIPMENT

Here's a list of all the equipment you will need in order to get baking:

+ Free-standing mixer with a paddle and whisk attachment, or a hand-held electric whisk (or a balloon whisk – but your arm may fall off!)
+ Piping bags or spoons and a palette knife
+ Plastic disposable boxes with lids
+ Digital scales for wet and dry ingredients
+ Sieve
+ Jug
+ Ladle
+ Mixing bowls with high sides
+ Spoons: teaspoons, dessertspoons, tablespoons, large metal spoon for folding
+ Baking trays
+ Muffin tray
+ Cooling rack
+ Greaseproof paper
+ Muffin/cupcake cases
+ Timer
+ Bowls: small for icings, large for mixing
+ Plastic disposable containers for storing icing

+ INGREDIENTS

Buttermilk

If you can't get buttermilk use a mix of Greek yoghurt and milk, in the proportions 50% Greek yoghurt to 50% milk.

Cocoa powder

I use 100% cocoa powder. If your cocoa powder isn't as strong as that, my great friend Sara (a fabulous baker) recommends a teaspoon of coffee dissolved in the liquid of the recipe to enhance the chocolate flavour. I've tried it and it works really well.

Eggs

Throughout the recipes I have used medium organic eggs, each weighing approximately 50g. Always make sure your eggs are at room temperature before you use them for baking. If you do not use your egg whites immediately they can be stored in the fridge for 4 days or frozen for 1 month. Use them to make meringues.

Chocolate

Dark chocolate

+ Select dark chocolate 85%

+ Green and Black's 72%

+ Menier chocolat patissier 70%

+ Bournville 39%

Milk chocolate

+ 29%–35%

White chocolate

+ 30%

Instead of melting chocolate over a saucepan of simmering water you can melt it in a microwave. 300g will take 1–2 minutes. If the chocolate is too thick, dilute it with a few teaspoons of vegetable oil, not water.

Icings

Cream cheese icing

The cream cheese icing in these recipes is very soft and delicious and works really well as a filling and topping for most whoopies and cupcakes. It keeps well for up to 4 days and can be used directly from the fridge.

Butter icing

This is great for moulding the wacky and celebration whoopies and sets well. It also doesn't discolour and keeps well without being refrigerated. Do not refrigerate before use because it goes hard.

Roll-out icing

Most supermarkets sell roll-out icing. It is so versatile when you are creating whoopie or cupcake characters. Think of it like Play Doh. When rolling it out, use icing sugar to dust your work surface. Use it quickly because it will dry out (like Play Doh) and crack.

Food colourings

I use bright food paste colours for a lot of the wacky whoopies and some of the others. The brands I use are Sugar Flair and Wilton. These can be bought on line from www.make awishcakeshop.co.uk or www.imaginativeicing.demon.co.uk. There are some natural food colourings on the market too, such as beetroot and spinach powder. The Spice Shop in Blenheim Crescent sells these online at www.thespiceshop.co.uk. You can also use fruit purées to colour your icings and sponges, but your sponges will take on the flavour of the purée and the colour won't be as intense as you get with commercially bought food paste. When colouring icing add the food colouring with the end of a spoon so as not to over do it.

Soda water

You can use sparkling mineral water instead of soda water.

CLASSIC WHOOPIES AND CUPCAKES

In this chapter you will find a collection of traditional and modern classic flavours, from basic vanilla and chocolate to the relatively modern red velvet. In the whoopie section I have included a traditional Lamington, for our Australian and New Zealand friends, as well as a classic American marshmallow fluff. I have also included traditional cake flavours, such as coffee, and converted popular puddings such as strawberry cheesecake and banoffee pie into whoopies. If you love the pub favourite sticky toffee pudding, you'll find that here too, converted into a cupcake.

WHOOPIES

CUPCAKES

CLASSIC VANILLA WHOOPIE

+Makes 8 whoopies (7–9cm across) +Prep 20 minutes +Cook 8 minutes

I was inspired to make a vanilla whoopie by the classic and much-loved Victoria sponge cake. The vanilla sponges are sandwiched with lightly whipped cream and raspberry jam, then dusted with icing sugar. Perfect with a fresh pot of Earl Grey tea and a girly gossip!

SPONGE

200g plain flour

1 level teaspoon
  bicarbonate of soda

50ml buttermilk

1 teaspoon good-quality
  vanilla extract or essence

80g butter

100g caster sugar

1 free-range egg (50g),
  beaten

FILLING

150ml double cream

50g raspberry jam

TOPPING

a dusting of icing sugar

Preheat the oven to 200°C/400°F/gas 6 and line a baking tray with grease-proof paper. Sieve the flour and bicarbonate of soda into a bowl. Mix the buttermilk with the vanilla and set aside.

Cream the butter and sugar together in a bowl, using a hand-held electric whisk (or in a free-standing mixer using the whisk attachment), until pale. Scrape down the bowl while whisking. Once the mixture is pale, slowly add the beaten egg a little at a time while continuing to whisk. Once the egg has been incorporated, fold in the wet and dry ingredients with a large metal spoon – use the 'figure of eight' action – keeping air in the mix until you have an even colour (do not over-mix). Pipe or spoon 16 x 4cm dollops (at least 4cm high) on to the baking tray, spacing them well apart to allow for spreading, and bake in the preheated oven for 8 minutes.

While the sponges are cooking, whip the double cream until it holds soft peaks. Take the sponges out of the oven and leave them to cool on the tray. When cool, lift them off with a fish slice. Sandwich them together with whipped cream and raspberry jam, and dust with icing sugar.

Newhaven Library
Tel: Renewals 0345 60 80 195

Borrowed Items 20/05/2019 12:01
XXX9453

Item Title	Due Date
Blue dog	08/06/2019
* Let's make whoopies! : meet the new cupcake on the block	10/06/2019
* Bags : the modern classics : clutches, hobos, satchels : more	10/06/2019

* Indicates items borrowed today
Thankyou for using this unit
www.eastsussex.gov.uk
10% off take away drinks when you
show this receipt
at La Baguette Shop, Rose Cafe and
Restaurant or Newhaven Coffee Shop
For enquiries 0345 60 80 196

BASIC CHOCOLATE WHOOPIE

+ Makes 8 whoopies (7–9cm across) + Prep 20 minutes | Cook 8 minutes + Decorate 5 minutes

This is the whoopie that made our bakery's name, described by my husband's office manager as 'little drops of heaven'. With a brightly coloured set topping contrasting with the chocolate sponge and tangy cream cheese filling, they have been tweeted around the world! I love them with bright water icing, or plain with no icing at all.

Preheat the oven to 200°C/400°F/gas 6 and line a baking tray with grease-proof paper. Sieve the flour, cocoa powder and bicarbonate of soda into a bowl. Mix the buttermilk with the vanilla and set aside.

Cream the butter and sugar together in a bowl, using a hand-held electric whisk (or in a free standing mixer using the whisk attachment), until pale. Scrape down the bowl while whisking. Once the mixture is pale, slowly add the beaten egg a little at a time while continuing to whisk. Once the egg has been incorporated, fold in the wet and dry ingredients with a large metal spoon – use the 'figure of eight' action – keeping air in the mix until you have an even colour (do not over-mix). Pipe or spoon 16 x 4cm dollops (at least 4cm high), spacing them well apart to allow for spreading, on to the baking tray and bake in the preheated oven for 8 minutes.

While the sponges are cooking, you can start to make the filling. Cream the butter and icing sugar together, then add the cream cheese and vanilla. Mix until the filling is smooth, but take care not to over-beat or it will become runny.

To make the topping, put the icing sugar into a bowl and add the water, a little at a time, stirring until you have quite a thick paste but one that is loose enough to pipe or spoon on to the whoopies. Add the colour paste, a little at a time, on the end of a spoon.

Take the sponges out of the oven and leave to cool on the tray. When cool, lift them off with a fish slice. Sandwich them together with the classic vanilla cream cheese filling and top with the bright coloured water icing. Sprinkles or hundreds and thousands are good too.

SPONGE
140g plain flour

40g cocoa powder

1 level teaspoon bicarbonate of soda

90ml buttermilk

1 teaspoon good-quality vanilla extract or essence

80g butter

140g soft light brown sugar

1 free-range egg (50g), beaten

FILLING
50g very soft butter

100g icing sugar, sifted

150g Philadelphia cream cheese

1 teaspoon good-quality vanilla extract or essence

TOPPING
140g icing sugar, sifted

2 tablespoons water

2–3mm bright food colour paste

RED VELVET WHOOPIE

+ Makes 8 whoopies (7–9cm across) + Prep 20 minutes + Cook 8 minutes + Decorate 5 minutes

This moist and delicious sponge is a dramatic red colour. It works as a base for a Hallowe'en Evil Whoopie face (page 208), a romantic Valentine whoopie with heart sprinkles (page 192), or the face of the Caterpillar on page 158.

SPONGE

180g plain flour

20g cocoa powder

1 level teaspoon
  bicarbonate of soda

60ml buttermilk

1 teaspoon good-quality
  vanilla extract or essence

2 tablespoons red liquid
  food colouring (Dr Oetker)

80g butter

150g soft brown sugar

1 free-range egg (50g),
  beaten

FILLING

50g very soft butter

100g icing sugar, sifted

150g Philadelphia
  cream cheese

1 teaspoon good-quality
  vanilla extract
  or essence

TOPPING

140g icing sugar

2 tablespoons water

2–3mm red food colour
  paste

multi-coloured sprinkles
  or silver balls

Preheat the oven to 200°C/400°F/gas 6 and line a baking tray with greaseproof paper. Sieve the flour, cocoa powder and bicarbonate of soda into a bowl. Mix the buttermilk with the vanilla and Dr Oetker food colouring and set aside.

Cream the butter and sugar together in a bowl, using a hand-held electric whisk (or in a free-standing mixer using the whisk attachment), until pale. Scrape down the bowl while whisking. Once the mixture is pale, slowly add the beaten egg while continuing to whisk. Once the egg has been incorporated, fold in the wet and dry ingredients with a large metal spoon – use the 'figure of eight' action – keeping air in the mix until you have an even colour (do not over-mix). Pipe or spoon 16 x 4cm dollops (at least 4cm high), spacing them well apart to allow for spreading, on to the baking tray and bake in the preheated oven for 8 minutes.

While the sponges are cooking, you can start to make the filling. Cream the butter and icing sugar together, then add the cream cheese and vanilla. Mix until the filling is smooth, but take care not to over-beat or it will become runny.

To make the topping, put the icing sugar into a bowl and add the water, a little at a time, stirring until you have quite a thick paste but one that is loose enough to pipe or spoon on to the whoopies. Add the colour paste, a little at a time, on the end of a spoon.

Take the sponges out of the oven and leave to cool on the tray. When cool, lift them off with a fish slice. Sandwich them together with the classic vanilla cream cheese filling and top with the bright coloured water icing and sprinkles or silver balls.

COFFEE AND CAPPUCCINO WHOOPIES

+ Makes 8 whoopies (7–9cm across) or 12 whoopies (4–5cm across)
+ Prep 20 minutes + Cook 8 minutes + Decorate 5 minutes

These are excellent for a mid-morning coffee break. You can also make mini-sized ones, which work really well as an after-dinner petit four.

Preheat the oven to 200°C/400 F/gas 6 and line a baking tray with grease-proof paper. Sieve the flour and bicarbonate of soda into a bowl. Mix the buttermilk with the Camp coffee and set aside.

Cream the butter and sugar together in a bowl, using a hand-held electric whisk (or in a free-standing mixer using the whisk attachment), until pale. Scrape down the bowl while whisking. Once the mixture is pale, slowly add the beaten egg a little at a time while continuing to whisk. Once the egg has been incorporated, fold in the wet and dry ingredients with a large metal spoon – use the 'figure of eight' action – keeping air in the mix until you have an even colour (do not over mix). To make the larger whoopies, pipe or spoon 16 x 4cm dollops (at least 4cm high) on to the baking tray, spacing them well apart to allow for spreading, and bake in the preheated oven for 8 minutes. For the smaller whoopies, pipe or spoon 24 x 3cm dollops (at least 3cm high) on to the baking tray and bake in the preheated oven for 6 minutes.

While the sponges are cooking, you can start to make the filling. Cream the butter and icing sugar together, then add the cream cheese and Camp coffee. Mix until the filling is smooth, but take care not to over-beat or it will become runny.

To make the coffee topping, put the icing sugar into a bowl and add the strong coffee, a little at a time, stirring until you have quite a thick paste but one that is loose enough to pipe or spoon on to the whoopies. For the cappuccino topping, whip the cream until it holds soft peaks.

Take the sponges out of the oven and leave to cool on the tray. When cool, lift them off with a fish slice. Sandwich them together with the coffee cream cheese filling. To make coffee whoopies, top with the coffee water icing and chocolate sprinkles. To make cappuccino whoopies, top with whipped cream and a dusting of drinking chocolate.

SPONGE

200g plain flour

1 level teaspoon
   bicarbonate of soda

70ml buttermilk

2 teaspoons Camp coffee

80g butter

150g caster sugar

1 free-range egg (50g),
   beaten

FILLING

50g very soft butter

100g icing sugar, sifted

150g Philadelphia
   cream cheese

1 teaspoon Camp coffee

TOPPING

For the coffee whoopie

140g icing sugar

2 tablespoons really
   strong coffee (made
   with 2 teaspoons instant
   coffee and 2 tablespoons
   boiling water)

dark and light chocolate
   sprinkles

*For the cappuccino
whoopie*

300ml double or
   whipping cream

drinking chocolate,
   for dusting

PEANUT WHOOPIE

+ Makes 8 whoopies (7–9cm across)   + Prep 20 minutes   + Cook 8 minutes

The whoopie for nut lovers. All you need to do to make this delicious treat is flavour a chocolate sponge with crunchy peanut butter and fold a chopped-up Snickers bar through some vanilla cream cheese filling. It can stand alone, without a topping.

SPONGE

140g plain flour

20g cocoa powder

1 level teaspoon
  bicarbonate of soda

60ml buttermilk

1 teaspoon good-quality
  vanilla extract or essence

50g butter

120g soft light brown sugar

50g crunchy peanut butter

1 free-range egg (50g),
  beaten

FILLING

40g very soft butter

80g icing sugar, sifted

120g Philadelphia
  cream cheese

1 teaspoon good-quality
  vanilla extract or essence

1 Snickers bar, chopped

Preheat the oven to 200°C/400°F/gas 6 and line a baking tray with grease-proof paper. Sieve the flour, cocoa powder and bicarbonate of soda into a bowl. Mix the buttermilk with the vanilla and set aside.

Cream the butter, sugar and peanut butter together in a bowl, using a hand-held electric whisk (or in a free-standing mixer using the whisk attachment), until pale. Scrape down the bowl while whisking. Once the mixture is pale, slowly add the beaten egg a little at a time while continuing to whisk. Once the egg has been incorporated, fold in the wet and dry ingredients with a large metal spoon – use the 'figure of eight' action – keeping air in the mix until you have an even colour (do not over-mix). Pipe or spoon 16 x 4cm dollops (at least 4cm high) on to the baking tray, spacing them well apart to allow for spreading, and bake in the preheated oven for 8 minutes.

To make the filling, cream the butter and icing sugar together. Add the cream cheese and vanilla. Mix until the filling is smooth, but take care not to over-beat or it will become runny. Place in a mixing bowl and fold in the chopped Snickers bar.

Take the sponges out of the oven and leave to cool on the tray. When cooled, lift them off with a fish slice. Sandwich them together with the peanut vanilla cream cheese filling.

AMERICAN MARSHMALLOW FLUFF WHOOPIE

+ Makes 8 whoopies (7–9cm across)   + Prep 20 minutes   + Cook 8 minutes   + Decorate 5 minutes

Our North American cousins love marshmallow, and after tasting this whoopie I can see why. It's a chocolate sponge studded with marshmallow pieces and filled and topped with bright pink marshmallow fluff, fudge, dulce de leche and chocolate chips. The colours look brilliant together, and I love the textures of squishy marshmallow and crunchy choc chips. Use regular marshmallows if you can't get the mini ones.

Preheat the oven to 200°C/400°F/gas 6 and line a baking tray with grease-proof paper. Sieve the flour, cocoa powder and bicarbonate of soda into a bowl. Mix the buttermilk with the vanilla and set aside.

Cream the butter and sugar together in a bowl using a hand-held electric whisk (or in a free-standing mixer using the whisk attachment), until pale. Scrape down the bowl while whisking. Once the mixture is pale, slowly add the beaten egg a little at a time while continuing to whisk. Once the egg has been incorporated, fold in the wet and dry ingredients including the marshmallow pieces, using a large metal spoon – use the 'figure of eight' action – keeping air in the mix until you have an even colour (do not over-mix). Pipe or spoon 16 x 4cm dollops (at least 4cm high) on to the baking tray, spacing them well apart to allow for spreading, and bake in the preheated oven for 8 minutes.

While the sponges are cooking, you can start to make the filling. Mix the American fluff with the chopped Fudge bar and marshmallow pieces.

Take the sponges out of the oven and leave to cool on the tray. When cool, lift them off with a fish slice. Drizzle half the dulce de leche over 8 of the sponges and top with half the American fluff mix and a sprinkling of chocolate chips. Put the rest of the sponges on top. Drizzle with the rest of the dulce de leche, top with the rest of the American fluff mix and finally sprinkle with more chocolate chips.

SPONGE

140g plain flour

40g cocoa powder

1 level teaspoon bicarbonate of soda

90ml buttermilk

1 teaspoon good-quality vanilla extract or essence

80g butter

140g soft light brown sugar

1 free-range egg (50g), beaten

50g mini marshmallows, cut into small pieces

FILLING AND TOPPING

100g pink American marshmallow fluff

1 Fudge bar, chopped

50g mini marshmallows, cut into small pieces

100g dulce de leche

100g dark chocolate chips

STRAWBERRY CHEESECAKE WHOOPIE

+Makes 8 whoopies (7–9cm across)   +Prep 20 minutes   +Cook 8 minutes

This is a very pretty pink sponge streaked with a white cheesecake mix. Once baked, fill this whoopie with fresh strawberries and strawberry cream. Ideal for a summer picnic in the park. Buy the strawberry purée ready-made, or make your own by puréeing ripe strawberries in a blender. You can also add a teaspoon of red food colour paste for a stronger colour.

SPONGE

200g plain flour

1 level teaspoon bicarbonate of soda

25ml buttermilk

1 teaspoon good-quality vanilla extract or essence

40ml strawberry purée

80g butter

150g caster sugar

1 free-range egg (50g), beaten

CHEESECAKE

200g cream cheese

60g icing sugar

1 teaspoon good-quality vanilla extract or essence

1 free-range egg (50g), beaten

FILLING

200ml double cream

40ml strawberry purée

400g fresh strawberries

TOPPING

icing sugar, sifted

Preheat the oven to 200°C/400°F/gas 6 and line a baking tray with grease-proof paper. Sieve the flour and bicarbonate of soda into a bowl. Mix the buttermilk with the vanilla and strawberry purée and set aside.

Cream the butter and sugar together in a bowl, using a hand-held electric whisk (or in a free-standing mixer using the whisk attachment), until pale. Scrape down the bowl while whisking. Once the mixture is pale, slowly add the beaten egg a little at a time while continuing to whisk. Once the egg has been incorporated, fold in the wet and dry ingredients with a large metal spoon – use the 'figure of eight' action – keeping air in the mix until you have an even colour (do not over-mix). Put the cheesecake ingredients into a separate bowl and blend with a whisk. With a fork roughly mix the sponge with the cheesecake so that you can still see the white of the cheesecake and the pink of the sponge. Pipe or spoon 16 x 4cm dollops (at least 4cm high) on to the baking tray, spacing them well apart to allow for spreading, and bake in the preheated oven for 8 minutes.

While the sponges are cooking, you can start to make the filling. Whip the cream, being careful not to over-whip it. Add the strawberry purée. Halve the strawberries.

Take the sponges out of the oven and leave to cool on the tray. When cool, lift them off with a fish slice. Lay the halved strawberries on 8 of the sponges, near the edge, so that they can be seen when the sponges are sandwiched together. Pipe or spoon on the strawberry cream. Put the rest of the sponges on top and dust with icing sugar. Place a whole strawberry on top just before serving.

TOFFEE BANOFFEE WHOOPIE

+ Makes 8 whoopies (7–9cm across) + Prep 20 minutes + Cook 8 minutes + Decorate 5 minutes

For those of you who are crazy about bananas, this is the whoopie take on a banoffee pie. A banana sponge, a toffee banana filling, whipped cream and a dusting of cocoa – delicious!

Preheat the oven to 200°C/400°F/gas 6 and line a baking tray with grease-proof paper. Sieve the flour and bicarbonate of soda into a bowl. Mix the buttermilk with the vanilla and mashed bananas and set aside.

Cream the butter and sugar together in a bowl, using a hand-held electric whisk (or in a free-standing mixer using the whisk attachment), until pale. Scrape down the bowl while whisking. Once the mixture is pale, slowly add the beaten egg a little at a time while continuing to whisk. Once the egg has been incorporated, fold in the wet and dry ingredients with a large metal spoon – use the 'figure of eight' action – keeping air in the mix until you have an even colour (do not over-mix). Pipe or spoon 16 x 4cm dollops (at least 4cm high) on to the baking tray, spacing them well apart to allow for spreading, and bake in the preheated oven for 8 minutes.

While the whoopies are baking you can make the filling and topping. Mix the dulce de leche with the mashed banana. Whip the cream until it holds soft peaks.

Take the sponges out of the oven and leave to cool on the tray. When cool, lift them off with a fish slice. Sandwich them together with the dulce de leche and banana filling. Pipe the whipped cream over the top and dust with cocoa powder.

SPONGE

200g plain flour

1 level teaspoon bicarbonate of soda

65ml buttermilk

2 bananas, mashed

80g butter

150g castor sugar

1 teaspoon good-quality vanilla extract or essence

1 free-range egg (50g), beaten

FILLING

200g dulce de leche

1 banana, mashed

TOPPING

300ml double cream

cocoa powder

THE LAMINGTON WHOOPIE

+Makes 8 whoopies (7–9cm across) +Prep 20 minutes +Drying time 3 hours

I couldn't write a cookbook without dedicating a recipe to all my friends from New Zealand and Australia, especially Brigitte, my wonderful head chef at the Crazy Baker. This is a great recipe for using up your leftover whoopie bases – strictly speaking, you should use vanilla bases, but do try them with another flavour if you like.

SPONGE
16 classic vanilla whoopie
  bases (see page 22)
500g desiccated coconut

TOPPING
For the chocolate syrup
400g icing sugar, sifted
100g cocoa powder
100ml milk
30g butter
or
For the strawberry syrup
500ml strawberry purée
50–100ml hot water
  (not boiling)

FILLING
300ml double cream

Make up your classic vanilla whoopie bases and let them cool. You can do this up to 2 days in advance.

For the chocolate syrup, combine the icing sugar and cocoa powder in a bowl. Heat the milk and butter until the butter has melted. Add the icing sugar mixture to the milk and butter and stir to a runny, dipping consistency. Put to one side to cool. For the strawberry syrup, add the hot water to the strawberry purée and mix until you have a runny, dipping consistency. Allow to cool. Put the desiccated coconut on a large plate.

Dip the whoopie bases into your chosen syrup and roll in the desiccated coconut until well covered. Place on a baking tray to dry for 3 hours or overnight.

When the whoopies are dry, whip the cream until it holds soft peaks and sandwich the halves together.

GINGERBREAD WHOOPIE

+Makes 12 whoopies (4–5cm across) +Prep 20 minutes +Cook 7 minutes +Decorate 10 minutes

At our café the gingerbread men go down a treat, so I have tweaked the recipe to make a delicious soft gingery whoopie sponge filled with a spiced cream cheese filling and topped with a smiley face. I think these work best when they are slightly smaller than the usual whoopie size. Of course, if you don't think so, you can always eat two!

Preheat the oven to 200°C/400°F/gas 6 and line a baking tray with grease-proof paper. Sieve the flour, spices and bicarbonate of soda into a bowl. Mix the buttermilk with the golden syrup and treacle and set aside.

Cream the butter, sugar and orange zest together using a hand-held electric whisk (or in a free standing mixer using the whisk attachment) until pale. Scrape down the bowl while whisking. Once the mixture is pale, slowly add the beaten egg a little at a time while continuing to whisk. Once the egg has been incorporated, fold in the wet and dry ingredients with a large metal spoon – use the 'figure of eight' action – keeping air in the mix. Keep folding until the mixture is an even colour (do not over-mix). Pipe or spoon 24 x 3cm dollops (at least 3cm high), spacing them well apart to allow for spreading, on to the baking tray and bake in the preheated oven for 7 minutes.

While the sponges are cooking, you can start to make the filling. Cream the butter, icing sugar, vanilla and orange zest together, then add the cream cheese and spices. Mix until the filling is smooth, but take care not to over-beat or it will become runny. For the white water icing topping, sift the icing sugar into a bowl and add the water, a little at a time, stirring until you have quite a thick paste but one that is loose enough to pipe or spoon on to the whoopies. For the yellow water icing topping, do the same but add the colour paste, a little at a time, on the end of a spoon.

Take the sponges out of the oven and leave to cool on the tray. When cool, lift them off with a fish slice. Sandwich the sponges together with the spiced cream cheese icing. Pipe or spoon white icing on the top of the whoopie, let it set for a few minutes, then pipe on a yellow smiley face.

SPONGE

190g plain flour

2 teaspoons ground ginger

2 teaspoons ground cinnamon

½ teaspoon mixed spice

1 level teaspoon bicarbonate of soda

40ml buttermilk

30g golden syrup

40g treacle

80g butter

70g soft dark brown sugar

zest of ½ an orange

1 free-range egg (50g), beaten

FILLING

50g very soft butter

100g icing sugar, sifted

1 teaspoon good-quality vanilla extract or essence

zest of ½ an orange

150g Philadelphia cream cheese

1 teaspoon ground cinnamon

1 teaspoon ground ginger

TOPPING

For the white water icing

140g icing sugar, sifted

2 tablespoons water

For the yellow water icing

140g icing sugar, sifted

2 tablespoons water

2–3mm yellow food colour paste

VANILLA CUPCAKE
+Makes 12 cupcakes +Prep 15 minutes +Cook 20 minutes +Decorate 15 minutes

Everyone has their favourite vanilla sponge recipe and this is mine. It's really easy to make and it works every time. This recipe can be used as the basis for so many other flavours. These cupcakes look pretty piped with swirls of pastel-coloured cream cheese topping, decorated with sprinkles.

SPONGE
175g self-raising flour

125g butter

175g caster sugar

2 free-range eggs (50g), beaten

1 teaspoon good-quality vanilla extract or essence

40ml milk

TOPPING
50g very soft butter

100g icing sugar, sifted

150g Philadelphia cream cheese

1 teaspoon good-quality vanilla extract or essence

2–3 mm food colour paste

sprinkles or hundreds and thousands

Preheat the oven to 180°C/350°F/gas 4 and put 12 paper cases into a muffin tray. Sieve the flour into a bowl.

Cream the butter and sugar in a bowl, using a hand-held electric whisk (or in a free-standing mixer using the whisk attachment), until pale. Scrape down the bowl while whisking. Once the mixture is pale, slowly add the beaten eggs and vanilla a little at a time while continuing to whisk. Once the eggs have been incorporated, fold in the flour and milk with a large metal spoon – use the 'figure of eight' action – keeping air in the mix until you have an even colour (do not over-mix). The mixture should be of dropping consistency. Spoon the mixture into the muffin cases, filling them halfway up, and bake in the preheated oven for 15–20 minutes, checking at 12 minutes. They should have risen and the top should feel springy. A wooden skewer stabbed into the sponge should come out clean.

While the cupcakes are cooking, you can start to make the topping. Cream the butter and icing sugar together and add the cream cheese and vanilla. Mix until the icing is smooth, but take care not to over-beat or it will become runny. Add the food colour paste, on the end of a spoon. Go easy, because the colours are very strong. You can always add more if you need to.

When the cupcakes are ready, take them out of the oven and leave them to cool in the tray. Fill a piping bag with the vanilla cream cheese topping and pipe swirls over the top of each cupcake. Finish with sprinkles or hundreds and thousands.

CHOCOLATE CUPCAKE

+ Makes 12 cupcakes + Prep 15 minutes + Cook 20 minutes + Decorate 15 minutes

This is a variation on the vanilla recipe on page 42, substituting cocoa powder for some of the flour.

Preheat the oven to 180°C/ 350°F/gas 4 and put 12 paper cases into a muffin tray. Sieve the flour and cocoa powder into a bowl.

Cream the butter and sugar in a bowl using a hand-held electric whisk (or in a free-standing mixer using the whisk attachment), until pale. Scrape down the bowl while whisking. Once the mixture is pale, slowly add the beaten eggs and vanilla a little at a time while continuing to whisk. Once the eggs have been incorporated, fold in the flour and milk with a large metal spoon – use the 'figure of eight' action – keeping air in the mix until you have an even colour (do not over-mix). The mixture should be of dropping consistency. Spoon the mixture into the muffin cases, filling them halfway up, and bake in the preheated oven for 15–20 minutes, checking at 12 minutes. They should have risen and the top should feel springy. A wooden skewer stabbed into the sponge should come out clean.

While the cupcakes are cooking, you can start to make the topping. Cream the butter, icing sugar and cocoa powder together and add the cream cheese. Mix until the topping is smooth, but take care not to over-beat or it will become runny.

When the cupcakes are ready, take them out of the oven and leave them to cool in the tray. Fill a piping bag with the chocolate cream cheese topping and pipe swirls over the top of each cupcake. Finish with bright-coloured or chocolate sprinkles or shaved dark chocolate.

SPONGE

125g self-raising flour

50g cocoa powder

125g butter

175g caster sugar

2 free-range eggs (50g), beaten

1 teaspoon good-quality vanilla extract or essence

40ml milk

TOPPING

50g very soft butter

80g icing sugar, sifted

20g cocoa powder

150g Philadelphia cream cheese

bright coloured or chocolate sprinkles or shaved dark chocolate

RED VELVET CUPCAKE

+Makes 12 cupcakes +Prep 15 minutes +Cook 20 minutes +Decorate 15 minutes

In the 1920s red velvet cake was a signature pudding at the Waldorf Astoria hotel in New York. In the 60s, according to an urban myth, when a wealthy customer asked a waiter for the red velvet cake recipe she was billed a rather large amount for it. She was so affronted that she spread the recipe in a chain letter. The sponge of this cake is dyed a deep chocolatey red with food colouring and cocoa powder, and the cake is topped with a white cream cheese frosting.

SPONGE

145g self-raising flour

30g cocoa powder

125g butter

175g caster sugar

2 free-range eggs (50g), beaten

1 teaspoon good-quality vanilla extract or essence

2 tablespoons milk

2 tablespoons red liquid food colouring (Dr Oetker)

TOPPING

50g very soft butter

100g icing sugar, sifted

150g Philadelphia cream cheese

1 teaspoon good-quality vanilla extract or essence

red sprinkles

Preheat the oven to 180°C/ 350°F/gas 4 and put 12 paper cases into a muffin tray. Sieve the flour and cocoa powder into a bowl.

Cream the butter and sugar in a bowl, using a hand-held electric whisk (or in a free-standing mixer using the whisk attachment), until pale. Scrape down the bowl while whisking. Once the mixture is pale, slowly add the beaten eggs and vanilla a little at a time while continuing to whisk. Once the eggs have been incorporated, fold in the flour, milk and red food colouring with a large metal spoon – use the 'figure of eight' action – keeping air in the mix until you have an even colour (do not over-mix). The mixture should be of dropping consistency. Spoon the mixture into the paper cases, filling them halfway up, and bake in the preheated oven for 15–20 minutes, checking at 12 minutes. They should have risen and the top should feel springy. A wooden skewer stabbed into the sponge should come out clean.

While the cupcakes are cooking, you can start to make the topping. Cream the butter and icing sugar together and add the cream cheese and vanilla. Mix until the topping is smooth, but take care not to over-beat or it will become runny.

When the cupcakes are ready, take them out of the oven and leave them to cool in the tray. Fill a piping bag with the vanilla cream cheese topping and pipe swirls over the top of each cupcake. Finish with red sprinkles.

COFFEE AND WALNUT CUPCAKE

+Makes 12 cupcakes +Prep 15 minutes +Cook 20 minutes +Decorate 10 minutes

My mother loves coffee cakes. When I was eleven I had a school friend to stay for the weekend and while my mother was at work we decided to make her a birthday cake. It was a bit of a disaster, because we took it out of the oven too early and it was still raw in the middle. Not to be deterred, we scooped the raw bit out, filled the hole with butter icing and topped it with walnuts. She loved it! Hmm...I'm a lot better at baking now, so I hope you enjoy these little coffee delights. It's much easier to control baking when the cakes are little, which is probably why cupcakes were such a success when American housewives started making them in the nineteenth century.

Preheat the oven to 180°C/350°F/gas 4 and put 12 paper cases into a muffin tray. Sieve the flour into a bowl.

Cream the butter and sugar in a bowl, using a hand-held electric whisk (or in a free-standing mixer using the whisk attachment), until pale. Scrape down the bowl while whisking. Once the mixture is pale, slowly add the beaten eggs and vanilla a little at a time while continuing to whisk. Once the eggs have been incorporated, fold in the flour, milk and Camp coffee with a large metal spoon – use the 'figure of eight' action – keeping air in the mix until you have an even colour (do not over-mix). Stir in the walnuts. The mixture should be of dropping consistency. Spoon the mixture into the paper cases, filling them halfway up, and bake in the preheated oven for 15–20 minutes, checking the cupcakes at 12 minutes. They should have risen and the top should feel springy. A wooden skewer stabbed into the sponge should come out clean.

While the cupcakes are cooking, you can start to make the topping. Put the butter into the bowl of an electric mixer with a third of the icing sugar and attach the whisk. Start the mixer on a slow speed and gradually add the rest of the icing sugar in two batches, adding the coffee after the second batch has gone in – this will make it easier to mix.

When the cupcakes are ready, take them out of the oven and leave them to cool in the tray. Place a good tablespoon of the coffee butter icing on top of each cupcake and spread with a palette knife, giving a rustic swirl effect. Top each cupcake with a walnut half.

SPONGE

175g self-raising flour

125g butter

175g caster sugar

2 free-range eggs (50g), beaten

1 teaspoon good-quality vanilla extract or essence

2 tablespoons milk

4 teaspoons Camp coffee

50g walnut pieces, chopped

TOPPING

100g unsalted butter, at room temperature

200g icing sugar, sifted

2 tablespoons really strong coffee (made with 2 teaspoons instant coffee and 2 tablespoons boiling water)

12 walnut halves

STICKY TOFFEE CUPCAKE

+Makes 12 cupcakes +Prep 15 minutes +Cook 20 minutes +Decorate 15 minutes

There are not many restaurants in England that don't have a sticky toffee pudding on the menu. I thought I would try it as a cupcake and it really works. The sponges must be really moist, so make sure you don't over-bake them. They are best eaten with a dessertspoon, as you would the pudding. Make the cakes early, before your friends arrive. Then pop them back into the oven for a few minutes to warm through before topping them with whipped cream and dulce de leche.

SPONGE

175g plain flour

1 level teaspoon
  bicarbonate of soda

150g chopped dates

60ml hot water

1 teaspoon good-quality
  vanilla extract
  or essence

4 teaspoons Camp coffee

75g butter

125g caster sugar

2 free-range eggs (50g),
  beaten

TOPPING

200ml double cream

100ml dulce de leche

Preheat the oven to 180°C/ 350°F/gas 4 and put 12 paper cases into a muffin tray. Sieve the flour and bicarbonate of soda into a bowl. Mix together the dates, hot water, vanilla and Camp coffee.

Cream the butter and sugar in a bowl, using a hand-held electric whisk (or in a free-standing mixer using the whisk attachment), until pale. Scrape down the bowl while whisking. Once the mixture is pale, slowly add the beaten eggs a little at a time while continuing to whisk. Once the eggs have been incorporated, fold in the flour and the date mixture with a large metal spoon – use the 'figure of eight' action – keeping air in the mix until you have an even colour (do not over-mix). The mixture should be of dropping consistency. Spoon the mixture into the paper cases, filling them halfway up, and bake in the preheated oven for 15–20 minutes, checking the cupcakes at 12 minutes. They should have risen and the top should feel quite soft. A wooden skewer stabbed into the sponge should come out clean.

When the cupcakes are ready, take them out of the oven and leave them to rest in the tray for 5 minutes. Meanwhile whip the cream until it holds soft peaks. Pipe cream over the top of each cupcake and drizzle with dulce de leche. Serve immediately.

CHOCOLATE WHOOPIES AND CUPCAKES

I have so many chocolate recipes that I just had to dedicate a whole chapter to chocolate. In fact I had so many ideas I couldn't fit them all in, so the ones included here are my absolute favourites. I have tried to include a variety of styles and methods to create different textures in the sponge. If you're a chocolate lover, I hope you enjoy all these.

WHOOPIES

CUPCAKES

DEVIL'S FOOD CAKE WHOOPIE

+Makes 8 whoopies (7–9cm across)   +Prep 10 minutes   +Cook 8 minutes   +Decorate 20 minutes

I have been making this devil's food cake for the last twenty years as a birthday cake, often in the shape of a train or a ship, and last weekend as a tank for my little boy Michael's seventh birthday. I thought it would make a really good whoopie and it does. With a chocolate fudge topping and a soured cream filling, it is just perfect, but if you find soured cream too sharp, use half soured cream and half whipped double cream.

SPONGE

130g self-raising flour

25g cocoa powder

1 level teaspoon
   bicarbonate of soda

130g caster sugar

25g soft butter

1 free-range egg (50g),
   beaten

50ml yoghurt

2 teaspoons milk

FILLING

100g soured cream

TOPPING

*For the chocolate
   fudge topping*

100g Bournville chocolate

100g caster sugar

100ml evaporated milk

2 teaspoons good-quality
   vanilla extract or essence

*For the white water icing
   (optional)*

140g icing sugar

3 tablespoons water

Preheat the oven to 200°C/400°F/gas 6 and line a baking tray with grease-proof paper.

This is so easy you can make it in a food processor. Put all the dry ingredients in first and blend for 10 seconds, then add all the wet ingredients. Blend for 5 seconds until just mixed (do not over-mix), then scrape down the sides of the processor bowl and blend for 2–3 seconds. You can also mix the dry ingredients with the wet ingredients using a hand-held mixer. Pipe or spoon 16 x 3cm dollops (at least 4cm high) on to the baking tray, spacing them well apart to allow for spreading, and bake in the preheated oven for 8 minutes.

While the sponges are cooking, you can start to make the chocolate fudge topping. Chop up the chocolate. Put the caster sugar and evaporated milk in a heavy-bottomed saucepan and bring to the boil. Boil rapidly for 5 minutes without stirring, being careful not to over-boil. The mixture should become thick. After 5 minutes add the vanilla and the dark chocolate and stir until melted. For the white water icing, if using, put the icing sugar into a bowl and add the water a little at a time until you have a paste that is loose enough to write with.

Take the sponges out of the oven and leave to cool on the tray. When cool, lift them off with a fish slice. Sandwich them together with soured cream. Spread each whoopie with the chocolate fudge topping, let it dry for a few minutes. If you want to have a little fun, you could pipe 'Little Devil' in white water icing on top.

TRIPLE CHOCOLATE WHOOPIE

+ Makes 8 whoopies (7–9cm across) + Prep 20 minutes + Cook 8 minutes + Decorate 5 minutes

This whoopie has a slightly more biscuity sponge, with milk and white chocolate taste explosions, and is one for chocoholics everywhere. The sponges are filled with a chocolate cream cheese icing, then topped with melted white chocolate and chocolate sprinkles or shavings.

Preheat the oven to 200°C/400°F/gas 6 and line a baking tray with grease-proof paper. Sieve the flour, cocoa powder and bicarbonate of soda into a bowl.

Cream the butter and both sugars together in a bowl, using a hand-held electric whisk (or in a free-standing mixer using the whisk attachment), until pale. Scrape down the bowl while whisking. Once the mixture is pale, slowly add the beaten egg and vanilla a little at a time while continuing to whisk. Once the egg has been incorporated, fold in the wet and dry ingredients with a large metal spoon – use the 'figure of eight' action – keeping air in the mix until you have an even colour (do not over-mix). Stir in the chocolate chips. Pipe or spoon 16 x 4cm dollops (at least 4cm high) on to the baking tray, spacing them well apart to allow for spreading, and bake in the preheated oven for 8 minutes.

While the sponges are cooking, you can start to make the filling. Cream the butter, icing sugar and cocoa powder together and add the cream cheese. Mix until the filling is smooth, but take care not to over-beat or it will become runny. Melt the white chocolate in a bowl over a saucepan of barely simmering water.

Take the sponges out of the oven and leave to cool on the tray. When cool, lift them off with a fish slice. Sandwich the sponges together with the chocolate cream cheese filling and top with the melted white chocolate. Finish with dark chocolate sprinkles.

SPONGE

130g plain flour

50g cocoa powder

1 level teaspoon bicarbonate of soda

120g butter

60g caster sugar

120g soft light brown sugar

1 free-range egg (50g), beaten

2 teaspoons good-quality vanilla extract or essence

60g white chocolate chips

60g milk chocolate chips

FILLING

50g very soft butter

80g icing sugar, sifted

20g cocoa powder

150g Philadelphia cream cheese

TOPPING

100g white chocolate

dark chocolate sprinkles

CHOCOLATE COCONUT WHOOPIE

+ Makes 8 whoopies (7–9cm across) + Prep 20 minutes + Cook 8 minutes + Decorate 10 minutes

The Bounty bar of whoopies! I absolutely love Bounties, so I really wanted to make a Bounty whoopie. The chocolate sponge has coconut in it, and a concentrated cream cheese coconut filling sandwiches the sponges together. It will transport you to the blue sea, palm trees and glorious white sand of a Caribbean island, even on a dreary winter day.

SPONGE

100g plain flour

40g cocoa powder

1 level teaspoon bicarbonate of soda

60g desiccated coconut

90ml buttermilk

1 teaspoon good-quality vanilla extract or essence

100g butter

140g soft light brown sugar

1 free-range egg (50g), beaten

FILLING

50g very soft butter

75g desiccated coconut

100g Philadelphia cream cheese

20ml milk

TOPPING

100g milk chocolate (30% cocoa solids)

50g desiccated coconut

Preheat the oven to 200°C/400°F/gas 6 and line a baking tray with grease-proof paper. Sieve the flour, cocoa powder and bicarbonate of soda into a bowl and stir in the coconut. Mix the buttermilk with the vanilla and set aside.

Cream the butter and sugar together in a bowl, using a hand-held electric whisk (or in a free-standing mixer using the whisk attachment), until pale. Scrape down the bowl while whisking. Once the mixture is pale, slowly add the beaten egg a little at a time while continuing to whisk. Once the egg has been incorporated, fold in the wet and dry ingredients with a large metal spoon – use the 'figure of eight' action – keeping air in the mix until you have an even colour (do not over-mix). Pipe or spoon 16 x 4cm dollops (at least 4cm high) on to the baking tray, spacing them well apart to allow for spreading, and bake in the preheated oven for 8 minutes.

While the sponges are cooking, you can start to make the filling. Cream the butter and coconut together, then add the cream cheese. Mix until the filling is smooth, adding the milk if you need it, but take care not to over-beat or it will become runny. To make the topping, melt the milk chocolate in a bowl over a saucepan of barely simmering water.

Take the sponges out of the oven and leave to cool on the tray. When cool, lift them off with a fish slice. Sandwich the sponges together with the coconut cream cheese filling and pour the melted milk chocolate over the top. Sprinkle with a little desiccated coconut if required.

DARK CHOCOLATE WHOOPIE

+Makes 16 whoopies (3–4cm across) +Prep 25 minutes +Cook 5 minutes +Decorate 15 minutes

This is the whoopie for those sophisticated posh chocolate lovers who buy really bitter chocolate. These whoopies are so rich in flavour that I decided to make them in mini size. I think they would work really well as a petit four, with different essences like jasmine, violet or lavender in the chocolate ganache and a topping of crystallized rose petals, lavender or violets on top. Alternatively you could use herbs like thyme or rosemary to complement the essence. I have kept them plain here, but feel free to play.

Preheat the oven to 200°C/400°F/gas 6 and line a baking tray with grease-proof paper. Sieve the flour and bicarbonate of soda into a bowl. Melt the chocolate and half the butter in a bowl over a pan of barely simmering water.

Cream the sugar and the rest of the butter using a hand-held electric whisk (or in a free-standing mixer using the whisk attachment), until pale. Scrape down the bowl while whisking. Once the mixture is pale, slowly add the beaten egg and vanilla a little at a time while continuing to whisk. Once the egg has been incorporated, fold in the melted chocolate and dry ingredients with a large metal spoon – use the 'figure of eight' action – keeping air in the mix until you have an even colour (do not over-mix). If you decide to try using essences or herbs, add a few drops of essence or a few chopped leaves of a herb of your choice at this stage. Pipe or spoon 32 x 2cm dollops (at least 2cm high) on to the baking tray, spacing them well apart to allow for spreading, and bake in the preheated oven for 5 minutes.

While the sponges are cooking, make the filling. Break the chocolate into small pieces. Heat the cream in a saucepan, then take the pan off the heat and add the broken chocolate. Stir until the chocolate is incorporated into the cream, adding a flavour of your choice if you like. To make the topping, melt the chocolate in a bowl over a pan of barely simmering water.

Take the sponges out of the oven and leave to cool on the tray. When cool, lift them off with a fish slice. Sandwich them together with the chocolate ganache filling and drizzle over the melted dark chocolate.

SPONGE

100g plain flour

1 level teaspoon
  bicarbonate of soda

80g chocolate
  (70% cocoa solids)

80g butter

100g soft light brown sugar

1 free-range egg (50g),
  beaten

1 teaspoon good-quality
  vanilla extract or essence

FILLING

150g really dark chocolate
  (85% cocoa solids)

150g double cream

TOPPING

150g dark chocolate
  (85% cocoa solids)

BROWNIE WHOOPIE

+ Makes 8 whoopies (7–9cm across) + Prep 20 minutes + Cook 7 minutes

One of my catering clients books a supply of my brownies every year, so I thought I should try making a brownie whoopie. Since the whoopie sponge has to be quite firm, it took me a few attempts to get it right. In my view, a brownie should be soft and squidgy inside and crisp on the outside, so they need only 7 minutes in the oven, not the usual 8. I have made these whoopies slightly smaller than usual, as they are very chocolatey and rich, and filled them with a slightly sharper vanilla cream cheese. They are rich enough not to need a topping.

SPONGE

100g plain flour

100g cocoa powder

1 level teaspoon
  bicarbonate of soda

2 free-range eggs (50g),
  beaten

1 teaspoon good-quality
  vanilla extract or essence

100g butter

140g soft light brown sugar

FILLING

50g very soft butter

80g icing sugar, sifted

150g Philadelphia
  cream cheese

1 teaspoon good-quality
  vanilla extract or essence

Preheat the oven to 200°C/400°F/gas 6 and line a baking tray with grease-proof paper. Sieve the flour, cocoa powder and bicarbonate of soda into a bowl.

Cream the butter and sugar together in a bowl using a hand-held electric whisk (or in a free-standing mixer using the whisk attachment), until pale. Scrape down the bowl while whisking. Once the mixture is pale, slowly add the beaten eggs and vanilla a little at a time while continuing to whisk. Once the eggs have been incorporated, fold in the wet and dry ingredients with a large metal spoon – use the 'figure of eight' action – keeping air in the mix until you have an even colour (do not over-mix). The mixture will be quite stiff. Pipe or spoon 16 x 4cm dollops (at least 4cm high) on to the baking tray, spacing them well apart to allow for spreading, and bake in the preheated oven for 7 minutes.

While the sponges are cooking, you can start to make the filling. Cream the butter and icing sugar together, then add the cream cheese and vanilla. Mix until the filling is smooth, but take care not to over-beat or it will become runny.

Take the sponges out of the oven and leave to cool on the tray. When cool, lift them off with a fish slice. Sandwich the sponges together with the classic cream cheese filling.

CHOCOLATE ORANGE WHOOPIE

+ Makes 8 whoopies (7–9cm across) + Prep 2½ hours + Cook 8 minutes

I love the flavour combination of chocolate and orange, so I have used a chocolate orange mousse to fill these whoopies. Top them off with a piece of caramelized orange. You will need to make this before you start on the whoopies – alternatively you can buy dried orange slices from a good health food shop.

First make the caramelized orange for the topping. Preheat the oven to 150°C/300°F/gas 2. Thinly slice the orange and halve the slices. Put them on a baking tray and sprinkle them with caster sugar. Bake in the oven for 2 hours, checking after 1 hour and watching that the oranges caramelize but do not burn. Remove from the oven and leave the orange slices to cool on a wire rack or a sheet of greaseproof paper.

While the oranges are caramelizing, make the filling, so that it has time to set. Melt the chocolate in a bowl over a saucepan of simmering water. While it is melting, put all 6 egg whites into a clean dry bowl and whisk until the soft peak stage. Mix the egg yolks and orange zest with the melted chocolate, then fold in the egg whites a quarter at a time. Put into the fridge and leave to set for 2 hours.

Preheat the oven to 200°C/400°F/gas 6. Sieve the flour, cocoa powder and bicarbonate of soda into a bowl. Mix the buttermilk with the orange zest.

Cream the butter and sugar together in a bowl, using a hand-held electric whisk (or in a free-standing mixer using the whisk attachment), until pale. Scrape down the bowl while whisking. Once the mixture is pale, slowly add the beaten egg a little at a time while continuing to whisk. Once the egg has been incorporated, fold in the wet and dry ingredients with a large metal spoon – use the 'figure of eight' action – keeping air in the mix until you have an even colour (do not over-mix). Pipe or spoon 16 x 4cm dollops (at least 4cm high) on to the baking tray, spacing them well apart to allow for spreading, and bake in the preheated oven for 8 minutes.

Take the sponges out of the oven and leave to cool on the tray. When cool, lift them off with a fish slice. Sandwich them together with most of the chocolate mousse filling. Place a little blob of mousse on top of each whoopie and top with a piece of caramelized orange.

SPONGE

140g plain flour

40g cocoa powder

1 level teaspoon bicarbonate of soda

90ml buttermilk

zest of 1 large orange

80g butter

140g soft light brown sugar

1 free-range egg (50g), beaten

FILLING

200g dark chocolate

4 free-range eggs (50g), separated

2 free-range egg whites (50g)

zest of 1 large orange

TOPPING

1 large orange

caster sugar

CHOCOLATE HAZELNUT WHOOPIE

+ Makes 8 whoopies (7–9cm across) + Prep 25 minutes + Cook 8 minutes + Decorate 5 minutes

When I was pregnant I ate Nutella out of the jar by the spoonful – that's probably why I had ten-pound babies! So here's one for any pregnant ladies who have the same craving.

SPONGE

100g plain flour

20g cocoa powder

1 level teaspoon
  bicarbonate of soda

40g hazelnuts, chopped

90ml buttermilk

1 teaspoon good-quality
  vanilla extract or essence

80g butter

140g soft light brown sugar

1 free-range egg (50g),
  beaten

FILLING

50g very soft butter

50g icing sugar

50g Philadelphia
  cream cheese

100g Nutella

50g praline (see below)

TOPPING

100g Nutella

For the praline

100g caster sugar

100g toasted chopped
  hazelnuts

First make the praline for the topping. Place the sugar in a heavy-bottomed pan and heat until melted and caramelized. Add the hazelnuts and tip on to a greased baking sheet. Once cooled, break the praline into small pieces. You will need 50g for the filling and another 50g for the topping – keep the leftover praline to use another time. It will keep for about 2 weeks in an air-tight container.

Preheat the oven to 200°C/ 400°F/gas 6 and line a baking tray with grease-proof paper. Sieve the flour, cocoa powder and bicarbonate of soda into a bowl and stir in the hazelnuts. Mix the buttermilk with the vanilla and set aside.

Cream the butter and sugar together in a bowl, using a hand-held electric whisk (or in a free-standing mixer using the whisk attachment), until pale. Scrape down the bowl while whisking. Once the mixture is pale, slowly add the beaten egg a little at a time while continuing to whisk. Once the egg has been incorporated, fold in the wet and dry ingredients with a large metal spoon – use the 'figure of eight' action – keeping air in the mix until you have an even colour (do not over-mix). Pipe or spoon 16 x 4cm dollops (at least 4cm high) on to the baking tray, spacing them well apart to allow for spreading, and bake in the preheated oven for 8 minutes.

While the sponges are cooking, you can start to make the filling. Cream the butter and icing sugar together, then add the cream cheese. Mix until the filling is smooth, but take care not to over-beat or it will become runny. Stir in the Nutella.

Take the sponges out of the oven and leave to cool on the tray. When cool, lift them off with a fish slice. Sandwich them together with the Nutella cream cheese filling and a sprinkling of praline. Spoon Nutella over the top of each whoopie and finish with more praline.

MOCHA WHOOPIE

Chocolate and coffee in one hit. If you can't find chocolate-coated coffee beans, you can make them yourself by just dipping a coffee bean in melted chocolate.

Preheat the oven to 200°C/400°F/gas 6 and line a baking tray with grease-proof paper. Sieve the flour, cocoa powder and bicarbonate of soda into a bowl. Mix the buttermilk with the vanilla and coffee and set aside.

Cream the butter and sugar together in a bowl, using a hand-held electric whisk (or in a free-standing mixer using the whisk attachment), until pale. Scrape down the bowl while whisking. Once the mixture is pale, slowly add the beaten egg a little at a time while continuing to whisk. Once the egg has been incorporated, fold in the wet and dry ingredients with a large metal spoon – use the 'figure of eight' action – keeping air in the mix until you have an even colour (do not over-mix). Pipe or spoon 16 x 4cm dollops (at least 4cm high) on to the baking tray, spacing them well apart to allow for spreading, and bake in the preheated oven for 8 minutes.

While the sponges are cooking, you can start to make the filling. Cream the butter, icing sugar and cocoa powder together, then add the cream cheese and the coffee. Mix until the filling is smooth, but take care not to over-beat or it will become runny. For the topping, sift the icing sugar and cocoa powder into a bowl and add the coffee, a little at a time, stirring until you have quite a thick paste but one that is loose enough to pipe or spoon on to the whoopies.

Take the sponges out of the oven and leave to cool on the tray. When cool, lift them off with a fish slice. Sandwich them together with the mocha cream cheese filling and top each one with the mocha water icing and a chocolate-coated coffee bean.

SPONGE

140g plain flour

40g cocoa

1 level teaspoon bicarbonate of soda

70ml buttermilk

1 teaspoon good-quality vanilla extract or essence

2 tablespoons strong coffee (made with 2 teaspoons instant coffee and 2 tablespoons boiling water)

80g butter

140g soft light brown sugar

1 free-range egg (50g), beaten

FILLING

50g very soft butter

80g icing sugar, sifted

20g cocoa powder

150g Philadelphia cream cheese

2 tablespoons strong coffee (made with 2 teaspoons instant coffee and 2 tablespoons boiling water)

TOPPING

110g icing sugar

30g cocoa powder

2 tablespoons strong coffee (made with 2 teaspoons instant coffee and 2 tablespoons boiling water)

chocolate-coated coffee beans

BLACK FOREST WHOOPIE

+ Makes 8 whoopies (7–9cm across) + Prep 20 minutes + Cook 8 minutes + Decorate 10 minutes

We were only offered a term of cooking classes at school, so I jumped at the chance and insisted on making complicated things like chocolate soufflé. I also learnt how to make a Black Forest gâteau – a must at any 70s dinner party. Since we are having a bit of a retro revival at the moment, I thought a Black Forest whoopie would make a good twenty-first-century pudding. It's a really dark chocolate sponge filled with cherries, soaked in Kirsch, topped with cream and grated chocolate.

SPONGE

130g plain flour

50g cocoa powder

1 level teaspoon
    bicarbonate of soda

90ml buttermilk

1 teaspoon good-quality
    vanilla extract or essence

80g butter

140g soft light brown sugar

1 free-range egg (50g),
    beaten

FILLING

300ml double cream

1 x 400g tin of cherries

50ml Kirsch

TOPPING

200ml double cream

50g grated chocolate

Preheat the oven to 200°C/400°F/gas 6 and line a baking tray with grease-proof paper. Sieve the flour, cocoa powder and bicarbonate of soda into a bowl. Mix the buttermilk with the vanilla and set aside.

Cream the butter and sugar together in a bowl, using a hand-held electric whisk (or in a free-standing mixer using the whisk attachment), until pale. Scrape down the bowl while whisking. Once the mixture is pale, slowly add the beaten egg a little at a time while continuing to whisk. Once the egg has been incorporated, fold in the wet and dry ingredients with a large metal spoon – use the 'figure of eight' action – keeping air in the mix until you have an even colour (do not over-mix). Pipe or spoon 16 x 4cm dollops (at least 4cm high) on to the baking tray, spacing them well apart to allow for spreading, and bake in the preheated oven for 8 minutes.

While the sponges are cooking, drain the tinned cherries and put them into a bowl. Add 3 tablespoons of Kirsch. Whip the double cream for the filling and topping.

Take the sponges out of the oven and leave to cool on the tray. When cool, lift them off with a fish slice. Turn 8 of the sponge halves dome side down and top with the Kirsch-soaked cherries. Pipe or spoon on the whipped cream and put the rest of the sponge halves on top. Pipe some more whipped cream on top of each whoopie and finish with grated chocolate.

TIRAMISÙ 'PICK-ME-UP' WHOOPIE

+ Makes 8 whoopies (7–9cm across)   + Prep 20 minutes   + Cook 8 minutes   + Decorate 5 minutes

We are a household of tiramisù lovers, and the boys do say that my tiramisù is the best! The creamy filling is based on a northern Italian recipe for 'pick-me-up pudding'. If you're in need of a little pick-me-up, this whoopie should definitely help – the chocolate sponge is soaked in coffee and Tia Maria liqueur, with a creamy, chocolatey mascarpone filling

Preheat the oven to 200°C/400°F/gas 6 and line a baking tray with grease-proof paper. Sieve the flour, cocoa powder and bicarbonate of soda into a bowl. Mix the buttermilk with the golden syrup and set aside.

Cream the butter and demerara sugar together in a bowl, using a hand-held electric whisk (or in a free-standing mixer using the whisk attachment), until pale. Scrape down the bowl while whisking. Once the mixture is pale, slowly add the beaten egg a little at a time while continuing to whisk. Once the egg has been incorporated, fold in the wet and dry ingredients with a large metal spoon – use the 'figure of eight' action – keeping air in the mix until you have an even colour (do not over-mix). Pipe or spoon 16 x 4cm dollops (at least 4cm high) on to the baking tray, spacing them well apart to allow for spreading, and bake in the preheated oven for 8 minutes.

While the sponges are cooking, you can start to make the filling. Whisk the mascarpone, egg and brown sugar together and stir in the grated chocolate. For the topping, sift the icing sugar into a bowl and add the Tia Maria, a little at a time, stirring until you have quite a thick paste but one that is loose enough to pipe or spoon on to the whoopies.

Take the sponges out of the oven and leave to cool on the tray. When cool, lift them off with a fish slice. Mix the Tia Maria and coffee in a small bowl. Place the whoopie halves dome side down and drizzle with the Tia Maria and coffee mixture. Sandwich the sponges together with the tiramisù filling. Pipe or spread the Tia Maria topping over the whoopie and finish with grated chocolate.

SPONGE

140g plain flour

30g cocoa powder

1 level teaspoon bicarbonate of soda

60ml buttermilk

25g golden syrup

100g butter

100g demerara sugar

1 free-range egg (50g), beaten

40ml Tia Maria

40ml strong black coffee (made with 3 teaspoons instant coffee and 3 tablespoons boiling water)

FILLING

250g mascarpone

1 free-range egg (50g), beaten

50g soft brown sugar

50g grated dark chocolate (70% cocoa solids)

TOPPING

150g icing sugar

2–3 tablespoons Tia Maria

grated dark chocolate

SACHERTORTE WHOOPIE

+ Makes 12 whoopies (4–5cm across) + Prep 1½ hours + Cook 8 minutes + Decorate 30 minutes

The Sachertorte is a cake originally developed at the Hotel Sacher in Vienna. The cake is a chocolate mousse-like meringue. The sponges are layered with apricot jam and chocolate ganache, then coated with more chocolate ganache and finally a layer of dark chocolate. This recipe takes a bit more time than the others, but it makes the most amazing whoopie.

SPONGE

90g plain flour

15g cocoa powder

½ level teaspoon
    bicarbonate of soda

115g chocolate
    (70% cocoa solids)

70g butter

70g caster sugar

4 free-range eggs (50g),
    separated

120g icing sugar

FILLING AND TOPPING

apricot jam

For the chocolate ganache

450g dark chocolate

450ml double cream

For the chocolate coating

400g chocolate

First make the chocolate ganache for the filling and topping. Break the chocolate into small pieces. Heat the cream in a saucepan, then take the pan off the heat, add the chocolate and stir until it is incorporated into the cream. Put into the fridge for 30 minutes to set.

Preheat the oven to 200°C/ 400°F/gas 6 and line a baking tray with grease-proof paper. Sieve the flour, cocoa powder and bicarbonate of soda into a bowl. Melt the chocolate in a bowl over a pan of barely simmering water, or melt it in the microwave for 1 minute.

Cream the butter and sugar together in a bowl, using a hand-held electric whisk (or in a free-standing mixer using the whisk attachment), until pale. Scrape down the bowl while whisking. Once the mixture is pale, slowly add the egg yolks one at a time while continuing to whisk. In a separate bowl, whisk the egg whites until soft peaks appear, then add the icing sugar and continue whisking to make a meringue mixture. Fold the melted chocolate into the egg yolk mixture, then fold in the flour and meringue mixture alternately. Do not over-mix. Pipe or spoon 24 x 3cm dollops (at least 5cm high) on to the baking tray, spacing them well apart to allow for spreading, and bake in the preheated oven for 8 minutes.

Take the sponges out of the oven and leave to cool on the tray. When cool, lift them off with a fish slice. These sponges fall slightly while cooling, so don't worry if that happens. Spread a layer of apricot jam over half the sponges and a layer of chocolate ganache over the rest. Sandwich the two halves together. Then coat each whole whoopie in chocolate ganache so that it looks like a round ball of chocolate. Put them into the fridge for 30 minutes.

To make the final chocolate coating, melt the dark chocolate in a bowl over a pan of barely simmering water, or melt it in the microwave for 1 minute. Place the whoopies on a cooling rack and ladle over the melted chocolate. Let the coating set, then write 'Sacher' in melted chocolate on top of each whoopie.

JAFFA CUPCAKE

Makes 12 cupcakes + Prep time 2½ hours + Cook time 20 minutes + Decorate 10 minutes

This is so good that I'm thinking of entering it in next year's National Cupcake Competition. It has a very light orangey sponge topped with a layer of orange jelly, followed by a layer of dark chocolate and grated orange zest. So vibrant it will leap off the plate and into your mouth! I've given instructions for making the orange jelly yourself, but you can use bought orange jelly if you prefer, made up according to the packet instructions.

Preheat the oven to 180°C/350°F/gas 4 and put 12 paper cases into a muffin tray. Sieve the flour into a bowl and stir in the orange zest.

Cream the butter and sugar in a bowl, using a hand-held electric whisk (or in a free-standing mixer using the whisk attachment), until pale. Scrape down the bowl while whisking. Once the mixture is pale, slowly add the beaten eggs and orange essence a little at a time while continuing to whisk. Once the eggs have been incorporated, fold in the flour and milk with a large metal spoon – use the 'figure of eight' action – keeping air in the mix until you have an even colour (do not over-mix). The mixture should be of dropping consistency. Spoon the mixture into the paper cases, filling them halfway up, and bake in the preheated oven for 15–20 minutes, checking the cupcakes at 15 minutes. They should have risen and the top should feel springy. A wooden skewer stabbed into the sponge should come out clean.

Just before the cupcakes finish cooking, you can start to make the orange jelly topping. Soak the gelatine leaves in the orange juice. Put the water and sugar into a pan and heat until all the sugar has dissolved. Add the orange juice and gelatine leaves and stir until the gelatine has dissolved. Set aside to cool slightly.

When the cupcakes are ready, take them out of the oven and leave them to cool in the tray. Pour a layer of orange jelly 0.5cm deep over each cupcake and leave to set for 2 hours.

When the jelly is set, you can make the chocolate topping. Melt the dark chocolate in a bowl over a saucepan of barely simmering water and leave to cool slightly. Drizzle it over the jelly and set aside to cool completely. Do not refrigerate, though, otherwise the chocolate will go dull. When everything has set, finish with a sprinkling of grated orange zest.

SPONGE

175g self-raising flour

zest of 2 oranges

125g butter

175g caster sugar

2 free-range eggs (50g), beaten

1 teaspoon orange essence

40ml milk

TOPPING

For the orange jelly

100g caster sugar

100ml water

200ml fresh orange juice

6 leaves of gelatine

For the chocolate topping

100g dark chocolate (70% cocoa solids)

zest of 4 oranges

MISSISSIPPI MUD PIE CUPCAKE

+ Makes 12 cupcakes   + Prep 25 minutes   + Cook 10 minutes   + Decorate 15 minutes

This is one for the men – a really rich gooey chocolate cake, flavoured with coffee and whisky. I have chosen Jim Beam, which is quite a soft, sweet bourbon, but you can use any brand you like.

SPONGE

170g self-raising flour

100g cocoa powder

60g dark chocolate

170g soft butter

170g caster sugar

2 free-range eggs (50g), beaten

2 tablespoons coffee (made with 2 teaspoons instant coffee and 2 tablespoons boiling water)

4 tablespoons Jim Beam bourbon

TOPPING

170g dark chocolate (70% cocoa solids)

170g caster sugar

170g evaporated milk

100g butter

2 teaspoons good-quality vanilla extract or essence

4 tablespoons Jim Beam bourbon

dark chocolate sprinkles

Preheat the oven to 180°C/350°F/gas 4 and put 12 paper cases into a muffin tray. Sieve the flour and cocoa powder into a bowl. Melt the chocolate in a bowl over a pan of barely simmering water and set aside to cool slightly.

Cream the butter and sugar in a bowl, using a hand-held electric whisk (or in a free-standing mixer using the whisk attachment), until pale. Scrape down the bowl while whisking. Once the mixture is pale, slowly add the beaten eggs a little at a time while continuing to whisk. Once the eggs have been incorporated, fold in the flour alternately with the melted chocolate, coffee and bourbon, using a large metal spoon – use the 'figure of eight' action – keeping air in the mix until you have an even colour (do not over-mix). The mixture should be quite wet.

Spoon the mixture into the paper cases, filling them halfway up, and bake in the preheated oven for 8–10 minutes, checking them after 8 minutes. They should have risen but still be a little wet inside. A wooden skewer stabbed into the sponge should come out a bit chocolatey.

While the cupcakes are cooking, you can make the topping. Chop the dark chocolate. Put the caster sugar and evaporated milk into a heavy-bottomed pan and bring to the boil. Boil rapidly for 5 minutes without stirring, being careful not to over-boil. The mixture should thicken. After 5 minutes add the chopped chocolate and the butter and stir until melted. Finally add the vanilla and bourbon. Let the mixture cool slightly, until it becomes a bit tacky.

When the cupcakes are ready, take them out of the oven and leave them to cool in the tray. Spread each cupcake with the bourbon fudge topping and finish with dark chocolate sprinkles.

TRIPLE CHOCOLATE CUPCAKE

+ Makes 12 cupcakes + Prep 25 minutes + Cook 20 minutes + Decorate 10 minutes

These cupcakes have a dark chocolate sponge that is really light, studded with white and milk chocolate pieces.

Preheat the oven to 180°C/350°F/gas 4 and put 12 paper cases into a muffin tray. Sieve the flour and cocoa powder into a bowl.

Cream the butter and sugar in a bowl, using a hand-held electric whisk (or in a free-standing mixer using the whisk attachment), until pale. Scrape down the bowl while whisking. Once the mixture is pale, slowly add the beaten eggs and vanilla a little at a time while continuing to whisk. Once the eggs have been incorporated, fold in the flour and milk with a large metal spoon – use the 'figure of eight' action – keeping air in the mix until you have an even colour (do not over-mix). Stir in the chocolate chips. The mixture should be of dropping consistency. Spoon the mixture into the paper cases, filling them halfway up, and bake in the preheated oven for 10–12 minutes, checking at 10 minutes. They should have risen and the top should feel springy. A wooden skewer stabbed into the sponge should come out clean.

While the cupcakes are cooking, you can start to make the topping. Cream the butter, icing sugar and cocoa powder together and add the cream cheese. Mix until the topping is smooth, but take care not to over-beat or it will become runny.

When the cupcakes are ready, take them out of the oven and leave them to cool in the tray. Place a spoonful of the chocolate cream cheese icing on each cupcake and spread with a palette knife until smooth. Top with white, dark and milk chocolate chips or shavings.

SPONGE

125g self-raising flour

50g cocoa powder

125g butter

175g caster sugar

2 free-range eggs (50g), beaten

1 teaspoon good-quality vanilla extract or essence

40ml milk

60g milk chocolate chips

60g white chocolate chips

TOPPING

50g very soft butter

80g icing sugar, sifted

20g cocoa powder

150g Philadelphia cream cheese

white, dark and milk chocolate chips or shavings

CHOCOLATE BROWNIE CUPCAKE

+ Makes 6 cupcakes + Prep 25 minutes + Cook 15 minutes

This cupcake stands alone without a topping. It is soft and squidgy inside, while the top sinks slightly and cracks open like parched earth. The eggs and sugar need whisking for 10 minutes, so if you have a free-standing mixer, it will mean you can get on with other things.

SPONGE
100g plain flour
100g self-raising flour
150g butter
125g dark chocolate
3 free-range eggs (50g), beaten
200g caster sugar

Preheat the oven to 180°C/350°F/gas 4 and put 12 paper cases into a muffin tray. Sieve the flours into a bowl. Melt the butter and chocolate in a bowl over a pan of barely simmering water. Set aside to cool slightly.

Place the eggs and caster sugar in the bowl of a free-standing mixer and whisk for about 10 minutes, until the mixture is pale and thick. Alternatively you can use a hand-held mixer. Fold in the chocolate mixture and the sifted flours with a large metal spoon – use the 'figure of eight' action – keeping air in the mix until you have an even colour (do not over-mix). The mixture should be of dropping consistency. Spoon the mixture into the paper cases, filling them three-quarters full, and bake in the preheated oven for 15 minutes, checking the cupcakes at 10 minutes and turning the muffin tin round. They should be set on top but still soft in the middle.

When the cupcakes are ready, take them out of the oven and leave them to cool in the tray.

CHOCOLATE NEMESIS
WITH RASPBERRY CUPCAKE

+ Makes 12 cupcakes   + Prep 40 minutes   + Cook 50 minutes

I have been making the River Café Chocolate Nemesis cake since Rose Gray and Ruth Rogers's first cookbook was published in 1995. Here is a cupcake version, with raspberries in the base to cut the richness and a dollop of crème fraiche on top.

It's a great one to make for gluten-intolerant friends, since there is no flour in the recipe, and it makes a fantastic pudding for a smart dinner party.

Preheat the oven to 180°C/350°F/gas 4 and put 12 paper cases into a muffin tray.

Place a tea towel in the bottom of a baking tray large enough to take your muffin tray (this will stop the muffin tray moving around). Make a sugar syrup by boiling 165g of the sugar with the water until the sugar dissolves, then continuing to boil it until it goes slightly syrupy. Melt the chocolate and butter in a bowl over a pan of barely simmering water.

Beat the eggs with the remaining 85g of caster sugar in a free-standing electric mixer for 25 minutes, until light and fluffy. Mix the sugar syrup with the melted chocolate and fold into the egg mixture with a large metal spoon – use the 'figure of eight' action – keeping air in the mix until you have an even colour (do not over-mix). The mixture should be of dropping consistency. Place 3 raspberries in the base of each paper case and pour in the chocolate mixture, filling the cases to about three-quarters of the way up. Just before baking, pour hot water into the baking tray so that it comes halfway up the sides of the muffin tin. Bake in the preheated oven for 50 minutes, until the top is crisp and the mixture is set in the middle. Check the water level halfway through the baking time to see if the water needs topping up.

When the cupcakes are ready, take them out of the oven and leave them to cool in the tray. Place a large spoonful of crème fraîche in the middle of each cupcake, followed by a raspberry and a sprig of mint.

SPONGE
250g caster sugar
120ml water
400g chocolate
  (70% cocoa solids)
270g butter
6 free-range eggs (50g)
punnet of fresh raspberries

TOPPING
100g crème fraîche
12 raspberries
12 mint tips

MILK CHOCOLATE CUPCAKE

Makes 12 cupcakes + Prep 25 minutes + Cook 15 minutes + Decorate 5 minutes

I have to admit that I have a very unsophisticated palate when it comes to chocolate. I love milk chocolate. In fact it is my favourite. So here is a cupcake for me. I like to eat it with a cold chocolate milk shake. Don't let appearances put you off. It is chewy, milky and delicious.

SPONGE

100g plain flour

100g self-raising flour

125g milk chocolate

125g butter

2 free-range eggs (50g), beaten

200g caster sugar

TOPPING

100g milk chocolate

Preheat the oven to 180°C/350°F/gas 4 and put 12 paper cases into a muffin tray. Sieve the flours into a bowl. Melt the milk chocolate and butter in a bowl over a saucepan of barely simmering water.

Whisk the eggs and sugar in a bowl, using a hand-held electric whisk (or in a free-standing mixer using the whisk attachment), until pale. Scrape down the bowl while whisking. Once the mixture is pale, fold in the flour and melted chocolate alternately with a large metal spoon – use the 'figure of eight' action – keeping air in the mix until you have an even colour (do not over-mix). The mixture should be of dropping consistency. Spoon the mixture into the paper cases, filling them halfway up, and bake in the preheated oven for 12–15 minutes. The cupcakes should have risen and the top should feel springy. This cupcake is dense and chewy, so the inside will be a little bit tacky when a wooden skewer is inserted.

While the sponges are cooking, you can make the topping. Melt the chocolate in a bowl over a saucepan of barely simmering water.

When the cupcakes are ready, take them out of the oven and leave them to cool in the tray. Pour the melted chocolate over the cooled cupcakes and leave to set.

WHITE CHOCOLATE CUPCAKE

+ Makes 12 cupcakes + Prep 25 minutes + Cook 20 minutes + Decorate 10 minutes

Although milk chocolate is my favourite, I do also love white chocolate. Maybe I just fancied the Milky Bar kid when I was nine and that's why I married a ginger bloke. This white chocolate cupcake with its white chocolate icing is a bit more sophisticated than a Milky Bar, and a lot more sophisticated than my ginger bloke.

Preheat the oven to 180°C/350°F/gas 4 and put 12 paper cases into a muffin tray. Sieve the flour into a bowl. Melt the white chocolate in a bowl over a pan of barely simmering water.

Cream the butter, sugar and vanilla in a bowl using a hand-held electric whisk (or in a free-standing mixer using the whisk attachment), until pale. Scrape down the bowl while whisking. Once the mixture is pale, slowly add the beaten eggs a little at a time while continuing to whisk. Once the eggs have been incorporated, fold in the sifted flour alternately with the milk and the melted white chocolate using a large metal spoon – use the 'figure of eight' action – keeping air in the mix until you have an even colour (do not over-mix). The mixture should be of dropping consistency. Spoon the mixture into the paper cases, filling them halfway up, and bake in the preheated oven for 15–20 minutes, checking the cupcakes at 12 minutes. They should have risen and the top should feel springy. A wooden skewer stabbed into the sponge should come out clean.

While the cupcakes are cooking, you can start to make the topping. Melt the white chocolate in a bowl over a pan of barely simmering water and set aside to cool. Cream the butter and icing sugar together and add the cream cheese. Add the cooled white chocolate and beat really well. Mix until the topping is smooth, but take care not to over-beat or it will become runny.

When the cupcakes are ready, take them out of the oven and leave them to cool in the tray. Fill a piping bag with the white chocolate cream cheese icing and pipe swirls on top of each cupcake.

SPONGE

175g self-raising flour

120g white chocolate

125g butter

125g caster sugar

1 teaspoon good-quality vanilla extract or essence

2 free-range eggs (50g), beaten

50ml milk

TOPPING

100g white chocolate

50g very soft butter

50g icing sugar, sifted

100g Philadelphia cream cheese

FRUIT, VEGETABLE AND FLOWER WHOOPIES AND CUPCAKES

From flowers and fruit in spring and summer and vegetables and roots all year round, you can make delicious cakes. I have chosen a selection of fruit, flower and vegetable whoopies and cupcakes that can be made from ingredients you may have in your garden, or find when out walking in the countryside or rummaging in the vegetable drawer of the fridge.

WHOOPIES

CUPCAKES

LEMON MERINGUE WHOOPIE

+ Makes 8 whoopies (7–9cm across) + Prep 35 minutes + Cook 13 minutes + Decorate 15 minutes

Rather than showing you how to make a straight lemon-flavoured whoopie, I thought I'd elaborate on one of my husband Harry's favourite desserts. When it comes to the filling, I like my lemon curd quite sharp, so if you have a sweet tooth simply add 20g more sugar. Use a silicone whisk to stir the curd if you can, as metal can cause it to discolour.

SPONGE

50g plain flour

50g wholemeal flour

1 level teaspoon bicarbonate of soda

50g porridge oats

50ml buttermilk

25g golden syrup

100g butter

100g demerara sugar

1 free-range egg (50g), beaten

FILLING

zest of 2 lemons

juice of 3 lemons

100g caster sugar

100g soft butter

4 free-range eggs (50g)

2 free-range egg yolks (50g)

TOPPING

3 free-range egg whites (50g)

150g caster sugar

First, make the lemon curd filling. For this you need a glass bowl that will fit over a saucepan. Put the lemon zest, juice and sugar into the bowl, add the butter, eggs and egg yolks, and whisk together. Place the bowl over a pan of barely simmering water and stir until the lemon curd is thick and blended. Set aside to cool.

Preheat the oven to 200°C/400°F/gas 6 and line a baking tray with grease-proof paper. Sieve the flours and bicarbonate of soda into a bowl and stir in the porridge oats. Mix the buttermilk with the golden syrup and set aside.

Cream the butter and sugar together, using a hand-held electric whisk (or in a free-standing mixer using the whisk attachment), until pale. Scrape down the bowl while whisking. Once the mixture is pale, slowly add the beaten egg a little at a time while continuing to whisk. Once the egg has been incorporated, fold in the wet and dry ingredients with a large metal spoon – use the 'figure of eight' action – keeping air in the mix until you have an even colour (do not over-mix). Pipe or spoon 16 x 4cm dollops (at least 4cm high), spacing them well apart to allow for spreading, on to the baking tray. Bake in the preheated oven for 8 minutes.

While the sponges are cooking, you can start to make the meringue topping. Whisk the egg whites until they hold soft peaks. Add the caster sugar, a table-spoon at a time, and continue to whisk until the meringue is shiny and stiff.

Take the sponges out of the oven and leave to cool on the tray. Turn the oven down to 140°C/275°F/gas 1. When the sponges are cool, lift them off the tray with a fish slice. Lay 8 of the sponges on a baking tray, flat side down. Put a spoonful of lemon curd filling in the centre of each one, then pipe or spoon the meringue over. Pop the meringue-topped sponges into the preheated oven for 5 minutes, then turn the oven down to 100°C/225°F/gas ¼ and cook for another 5 minutes. Remove from the oven and leave to cool.

Lay the other 8 sponges flat side up and divide the rest of the lemon curd filling between them. Place the cooled meringue-topped sponges on top.

LIME AND CARDAMOM WHOOPIE

This whoopie sponge has a lovely subtle cardamom flavour that doesn't overpower the lime. It works incredibly well as a dessert following a spicy meal.

Preheat the oven to 200°C/400°F/gas 6 and line a baking tray with greaseproof paper. Sieve the flour and bicarbonate of soda into a bowl. Mix the buttermilk with the lime juice and set aside.

Cream the butter, sugar, lime zest and cardamom together in a bowl, using a hand-held electric whisk (or in a free-standing mixer using the whisk attachment), until pale. Scrape down the bowl while whisking. Once the mixture is pale, slowly add the beaten egg a little at a time while continuing to whisk. Once the egg has been incorporated, fold in the wet and dry ingredients with a large metal spoon – use the 'figure of eight' action – keeping air in the mix until you have an even colour (do not over-mix). Pipe or spoon 16 x 4cm dollops (at least 4cm high) on to the baking tray, spacing them well apart to allow for spreading, and bake in the preheated oven for 8 minutes.

While the sponges are cooking, you can start to make the filling. Cream the butter, lime zest and icing sugar together and add the cream cheese. Mix until the filling is smooth, but take care not to over-beat or it will become runny. For the topping, sift the icing sugar into a bowl and add the lime juice, a little at a time, stirring until you have quite a thick paste but one that is loose enough to pipe or spoon on to the whoopies. Stir in the lime zest.

Take the sponges out of the oven and leave to cool on the tray. When cool, lift them off with a fish slice. Sandwich them together with the lime cream cheese filling and top with the lime water icing.

SPONGE

170g plain flour

1 level teaspoon bicarbonate of soda

80ml buttermilk

zest and juice of 2 limes

80g butter

140g soft light brown sugar

2 cardamom pods, crushed and outer shells discarded

1 free-range egg (50g), beaten

FILLING

50g very soft butter

zest of 2 limes

100g icing sugar, sifted

150g Philadelphia cream cheese

TOPPING

140g icing sugar, sifted

2 tablespoons lime juice

zest of 2 limes

ORANGE WHOOPIE

I love orange as a flavour, and the colour is so vibrant and jolly. If you want to emphasize the colour, try adding a few millimetres of orange colour paste to the sponge and icing. This is a whoopie that will really cheer you up – it's like sunshine.

SPONGE

170g plain flour

1 level teaspoon
    bicarbonate of soda

80ml buttermilk

zest of 1 large orange

80g butter

120g caster sugar

1 free-range egg (50g),
    beaten

FILLING

50g very soft butter

zest of 1 orange

100g icing sugar, sifted

150g Philadelphia
    cream cheese

TOPPING

140g icing sugar

zest of 1 orange

2 tablespoons orange juice

Preheat the oven to 200°C/400°F/gas 6 and line a baking tray with grease-proof paper. Sieve the flour and bicarbonate of soda into a bowl. Mix the buttermilk with the orange zest and set aside.

Cream the butter and sugar together in a bowl, using a hand-held electric whisk (or in a free-standing mixer using the whisk attachment), until pale. Scrape down the bowl while whisking. Once the mixture is pale, slowly add the beaten egg a little at a time while continuing to whisk. Once the egg has been incorporated, fold in the wet and dry ingredients with a large metal spoon – use the 'figure of eight' action – keeping air in the mix until you have an even colour (do not over-mix). Pipe or spoon 16 x 4cm dollops (at least 4cm high) on to the baking tray, spacing them well apart to allow for spreading, and bake in the preheated oven for 8 minutes.

While the sponges are cooking, you can make the filling. Cream the butter, orange zest and icing sugar together and add the cream cheese. Mix until the filling is smooth, but take care not to over-beat or it will become runny. For the topping, sift the icing sugar into a bowl and add the orange zest. Add the orange juice a little at a time, stirring until you have quite a thick paste but one that is loose enough to pipe or spoon on to the whoopies.

Take the sponges out of the oven and leave to cool on the tray. When cool, lift them off with a fish slice. Sandwich them together with the orange cream cheese filling and top with the orange water icing.

APPLE AND CINNAMON WHOOPIE

+ Makes 8 whoopies (7–9cm across) + Prep 2 hours + Cook 8 minutes

From August through to November my family goes mushroom picking, and these spicy little cakes are a great accompaniment to a flask of tea after a morning trekking through the woods. If you're not a forager, they're just as good to take along to the park for elevenses, when the kids have finished on the climbing frame. Remember to allow time for making the caramelized apple slices.

First make the caramelized apple for the topping. Preheat the oven to 150°C/300°F/gas 2. Thinly slice the apple (preferably using a mandolin) crosswise, so you have whole slices, and lay them on a baking tray. Sprinkle them with the caster sugar and bake in the preheated oven for 2 hours, checking after 1 hour that they are caramelizing but not burning. Remove the tray from the oven, lift the apple slices with a fish slice, give them a twist and lay them on a baking tray to dry.

Preheat the oven to 200°C /400°F/gas 6. Sieve the flour, cinnamon and bicarbonate of soda into a bowl. Mix the buttermilk with the vanilla and set aside.

Cream the butter and sugar together in a bowl, using a hand-held electric whisk (or in a free-standing mixer using the whisk attachment), until pale. Scrape down the bowl while whisking. Once the mixture is pale, slowly add the beaten egg a little at a time while continuing to whisk. Once the egg has been incorporated, fold in the wet and dry ingredients with a large metal spoon – use the 'figure of eight' action – keeping air in the mix until you have an even colour (do not over-mix). Pipe or spoon 16 x 4cm dollops (at least 4cm high) on to the baking tray, spacing them well apart to allow for spreading, and bake in the preheated oven for 8 minutes.

To make the filling, whip the cream until it holds soft peaks, being careful not to over-whip it. Stir in the Calvados. For the topping, sift the icing sugar and cinnamon together.

Take the sponges out of the oven and leave to cool on the tray. When cool, lift them off with a fish slice. Sandwich them together with the Calvados cream, saving a bit for the top. Dust the finished whoopies with the cinnamon icing sugar and put a slice of caramelized apple in the centre of each, secured with a blob of Calvados cream.

SPONGE
170g plain flour

1 level teaspoon ground cinnamon

1 level teaspoon bicarbonate of soda

50ml buttermilk

1 teaspoon good-quality vanilla extract or essence

80g butter

120g caster sugar

1 free-range egg (50g), beaten

100g apples, grated

FILLING
300ml double cream

2 teaspoons Calvados

TOPPING
1 red apple

2 teaspoons caster sugar

50g icing sugar, sifted

1 level teaspoon ground cinnamon

CHERRY WHOOPIE
+ Makes 8 whoopies (7–9cm across)   + Prep 20 minutes   + Cook 8 minutes

My parents have a little cherry tree in their garden that produces bucketloads of the sweetest fruit. So I thought I would try making a whoopie using the fruit straight from the tree. With bursts of red cherry through the sponge and a vanilla cream cheese filling, just a dusting of icing sugar and a pair of shiny fresh cherries is all the topping you need.

SPONGE

170g plain flour

1 level tablespoon
bicarbonate of soda

30ml buttermilk

2 teaspoons Kirsch
(optional)

80g butter

140g caster sugar

1 free-range egg (50g),
beaten

100g stoned ripe cherries

FILLING

50g very soft butter

100g icing sugar, sifted

150g Philadelphia
cream cheese

1 teaspoon good-quality
vanilla extract or essence

TOPPING

50g icing sugar, sifted

8 pairs of fresh cherries

Preheat the oven to 200°C/400°F/gas 6 and line a baking tray with grease-proof paper. Sieve the flour and bicarbonate of soda into a bowl. Mix the buttermilk with the Kirsch, if using, and set aside.

Cream the butter and sugar together in a bowl, using a hand-held electric whisk (or in a free-standing mixer using the whisk attachment), until pale. Scrape down the bowl while whisking. Once the mixture is pale, slowly add the beaten egg a little at a time while continuing to whisk. Once the egg has been incorporated, fold in the wet and dry ingredients with a large metal spoon – use the 'figure of eight' action – keeping air in the mix until you have an even colour (do not over-mix). Fold in the cherries, but not too thoroughly – that way you will have bursts of colour in the sponge when it is cooked. Pipe or spoon 16 x 4cm dollops (at least 4cm high) on to the baking tray, spacing them well apart to allow for spreading, and bake in the preheated oven for 8 minutes.

While the sponges are cooking, you can make the filling. Cream the butter and icing sugar together and add the cream cheese and vanilla. Mix until the filling is smooth, but take care not to over-beat or it will become runny.

Take the sponges out of the oven and leave to cool on the tray. When cool, lift them off with a fish slice. Sandwich them together with the classic cream cheese filling, then simply dust with icing sugar and top each whoopie with a pair of cherries.

CARROT WHOOPIE

+ Makes 10 whoopies (7–9cm across) + Prep 20 minutes + Cook 8 minutes

When sugar was rationed during the Second World War, carrots were often used as a sweetener for cakes. This is such an easy recipe – just mix the dry ingredients with the wet ingredients and there you have it! A simple zingy orange cream cheese filling complements the spicy sponge.

Preheat the oven to 200°C/400°F/gas 6 and line a baking tray with grease-proof paper. Sieve the flour, bicarbonate of soda, cinnamon and nutmeg into a bowl and stir in the sugar, walnuts and grated carrots. In another bowl beat the eggs and add the oil and vanilla. Fold the wet ingredients into the dry ingredients with a large metal spoon – use the 'figure of eight' action – keeping air in the mix until you have an even colour (do not over-mix). Pipe or spoon 20 x 4cm dollops (at least 4cm high) on to the baking tray, spacing them well apart to allow for spreading, and bake in the preheated oven for 8 minutes.

While the sponges are cooking, you can start to make the filling. Cream the butter, icing sugar and orange zest together and add the cream cheese. Mix until the filling is smooth, but take care not to over beat or it will become runny.

Take the sponges out of the oven and leave to cool on the tray. When cool, lift them off with a fish slice. Sandwich them together with the orange cream cheese filling and dust each whoopie with icing sugar.

SPONGE

175g self-raising flour

1 level teaspoon bicarbonate of soda

1 level teaspoon ground cinnamon

½ level teaspoon grated nutmeg

225g caster sugar

100g walnuts, chopped

200g carrots, finely grated

2 free-range eggs (50g), beaten

120ml sunflower oil

1 teaspoon good-quality vanilla extract or essence

FILLING

50g very soft butter

100g icing sugar, sifted

zest of 1 large orange

150g Philadelphia cream cheese

TOPPING

50g icing sugar, sifted

BEETROOT WHOOPIE

+ Makes 8 whoopies (7–9cm across) + Prep 20 minutes + Cook 8 minutes

The Poles love beetroot – it is incredibly healthy, rich in vitamins and minerals, and is also known as the vitality plant. This whoopie gains much of its sweetness from the beetroot. As it cooks, the grated beetroot creates a beautiful marbled effect in the sponge, so I have filled this whoopie with a burgundy vanilla cream cheese icing and left the top undusted.

SPONGE

180g plain flour

1 level teaspoon
  bicarbonate of soda

30ml buttermilk

200g cooked beetroot,
  grated

60g butter

60g soft light brown sugar

1 free-range egg (50g),
  beaten

FILLING

50g very soft butter

100g icing sugar, sifted

150g Philadelphia cream
  cheese

1 teaspoon good-quality
  vanilla extract
  or essence

2–3mm burgundy food
  colour paste

Preheat the oven to 200°C/400°F/gas 6 and line a baking tray with grease-proof paper. Sieve the flour and bicarbonate of soda into a bowl. Mix the buttermilk with the grated beetroot and set aside.

Cream the butter and sugar together in a bowl, using a hand-held electric whisk (or in a free-standing mixer using the whisk attachment), until pale. Scrape down the bowl while whisking. Once the mixture is pale, slowly add the beaten egg a little at a time while continuing to whisk. Once the egg has been incorporated, fold in the wet and dry ingredients with a large metal spoon – use the 'figure of eight' action – keeping air in the mix until you have an even colour (do not over-mix). Pipe or spoon 16 x 4cm dollops (at least 4cm high) on to the baking tray, spacing them well apart to allow for spreading, and bake in the preheated oven for 8 minutes.

While the sponges are cooking, you can start to make the filling. Cream the butter and icing sugar together, then add the cream cheese and vanilla. Mix until the filling is smooth, but take care not to over-beat or it will become runny. Add the colour paste, a little at a time, on the end of a spoon. For the topping, sift the icing sugar into a bowl and add the water, a little at a time, stirring until you have quite a thick paste but one that is loose enough to pipe or spoon on to the whoopies. Add the colour paste, a little at a time, on the end of a spoon.

Take the sponges out of the oven and leave to cool on the tray. When cool, lift them off with a fish slice. Sandwich them together with the burgundy cream cheese filling.

ROSE WHOOPIE

+ Makes 8 whoopies (7–9cm across) + Prep 20 minutes + Cook 8 minutes + Decorate 10 minutes

This whoopie is thoroughly pink, from the Turkish delight filling to the rose-water topping and the petals from the roses that grow in my garden.

Preheat the oven to 200°C/400°F/gas 6 and line a baking tray with grease-proof paper. Sieve the flour and bicarbonate of soda into a bowl. Mix the buttermilk with the rosewater and pink food colouring and set aside.

Cream the butter and sugar together in a bowl, using a hand-held electric whisk (or in a free-standing mixer using the whisk attachment), until pale. Scrape down the bowl while whisking. Once the mixture is pale, slowly add the beaten egg a little at a time while continuing to whisk. Once the egg has been incorporated, fold in the wet and dry ingredients with a large metal spoon – use the 'figure of eight' action – keeping air in the mix until you have an even colour (do not over mix). Pipe or spoon 10 x 4cm dollops (at least 4cm high) on to the baking tray, spacing them well apart to allow for spreading, and bake in the preheated oven for 8 minutes.

While the sponges are cooking, you can start to make the filling. Cream the butter and icing sugar together and add the cream cheese and rosewater. Mix until the filling is smooth, but take care not to over-beat or it will become runny. Add the colour paste, a little at a time, on the end of a spoon. Fold in the chopped Turkish delight. For the topping, sift the icing sugar into a bowl and add the rosewater, a little at a time, stirring until you have quite a thick paste but one that is loose enough to pipe or spoon on to the whoopies. Add the colour paste, a little at a time, on the end of a spoon.

Take the sponges out of the oven and leave to cool on the tray. When cool, lift them off with a fish slice. Sandwich them together with the rose cream cheese filling, and top with the rosewater icing and rose petals.

SPONGE

170g plain flour

1 level teaspoon bicarbonate of soda

80ml buttermilk

1 tablespoon rosewater

1 teaspoon pink liquid food colouring

80g butter

140g soft light brown sugar

1 free-range egg (50g), beaten

FILLING

50g very soft butter

100g icing sugar, sifted

150g Philadelphia cream cheese

1 teaspoon rosewater

2–3mm pink food colour paste

50g rose Turkish delight, cut into little cubes

TOPPING

140g icing sugar

2 tablespoons rosewater

2–3mm pink food colour paste

fresh rose petals

LAVENDER WHOOPIE
+ Makes 8 whoopies (7–9cm across)   + Prep 20 minutes   + Cook 8 minutes   + Decorate 10 minutes

Pat, the head chef at the Mitre gastropub in Holland Park in London, asked me to develop a lavender cake for his afternoon teas, and this is what I came up with: a lavender-flavoured sponge and filling, a white lemon-flavoured topping and a sprig of lavender to top it off. Perfect for an afternoon tea party.

SPONGE

140g plain flour

1 level teaspoon bicarbonate of soda

90ml buttermilk

1 teaspoon good-quality vanilla extract or essence

80g butter

140g soft light brown sugar

10g lavender flowers

1 free-range egg (50g), beaten

FILLING

50g very soft butter

100g icing sugar, sifted

150g Philadelphia cream cheese

flowers from a few sprigs of lavender

TOPPING

140g icing sugar

juice of 1 lemon

a few sprigs of lavender

Preheat the oven to 200°C/400°F/gas 6 and line a baking tray with grease-proof paper. Sieve the flour and bicarbonate of soda into a bowl. Mix the buttermilk with the vanilla and set aside.

Cream the butter and sugar together in a bowl with the lavender flowers, using a hand-held electric whisk (or in a free-standing mixer using the whisk attachment), until pale. Scrape down the bowl while whisking. Once the mixture is pale, slowly add the beaten egg a little at a time while continuing to whisk. Once the egg has been incorporated, fold in the wet and dry ingredients with a large metal spoon – use the 'figure of eight' action – keeping air in the mix until you have an even colour (do not over-mix). Pipe or spoon 16 x 4cm dollops (at least 4cm high) on to the baking tray, spacing them well apart to allow for spreading, and bake in the preheated oven for 8 minutes.

While the sponges are cooking, you can start to make the filling. Cream the butter and icing sugar together and add the cream cheese and lavender flowers. Mix until the filling is smooth, but take care not to over-beat or it will become runny. For the topping, sift the icing sugar into a bowl and add the lemon juice, a little at a time, stirring until you have quite a thick paste but one that is loose enough to pipe or spoon on to the whoopies.

Take the sponges out of the oven and leave to cool on the tray. When cool, lift them off with a fish slice. Sandwich them together with the lavender cream cheese filling and top with the lemon water icing. Finish with a sprig of lavender.

LEMONGRASS AND GINGER WHOOPIE
+ Makes 8 whoopies (7–9cm across) + Prep 20 minutes + Cook 8 minutes

Lemongrass and ginger complement each other so well in this whoopie. I have contrasted the sponge with a deliciously light lychee filling. This would be the perfect pudding after a Friday night Chinese.

Preheat the oven to 200°C/400°F/gas 6 and line a baking tray with grease-proof paper. Sieve the flour, ginger and bicarbonate of soda into a bowl. Mix the buttermilk with the cordial and set aside.

Cream the butter and sugar together in a bowl, using a hand-held electric whisk (or in a free-standing mixer using the whisk attachment), until pale. Scrape down the bowl while whisking. Once the mixture is pale, slowly add the beaten egg a little at a time while continuing to whisk. Once the egg has been incorporated, fold in the wet and dry ingredients, including the stem ginger, with a large metal spoon – use the 'figure of eight' action – keeping air in the mix until you have an even colour (do not over-mix). Pipe or spoon 16 x 4cm dollops (at least 4cm high) on to the baking tray, spacing them well apart to allow for spreading, and bake in the preheated oven for 8 minutes.

While the sponges are cooking, you can start to make the filling. Cream the butter and icing sugar together and add the cream cheese. Mix until the filling is smooth, but take care not to over-beat or it will become runny. Fold in the chopped lychees.

Take the sponges out of the oven and leave to cool on the tray. When cool, lift them off with a fish slice. Sandwich them together with the lemon-grass and ginger cream cheese filling.

SPONGE

170g plain flour

1 level teaspoon
  ground ginger

1 level teaspoon
  bicarbonate of soda

90ml buttermilk

2 teaspoons lemongrass
  and ginger cordial

80g butter

120g caster sugar

1 free-range egg (50g),
  beaten

50g stem ginger

FILLING

50g very soft butter

100g icing sugar, sifted

150g Philadelphia
  cream cheese

1 x 400g tin of lychees,
  drained and chopped

LEMON DRIZZLE CUPCAKE

+Makes 12 cupcakes   +Prep 20 minutes   +Cook 20 minutes   +Decorate 15 minutes

The British Baker is a trade magazine that my bakery started to subscribe to last June. I noticed that they were holding a National Cupcake Competition, so we entered, and this is our 2009 cupcake competition winner! It's a very lemony moist sponge with a very lemony swirly topping, finished off with a little gold ball.

SPONGE

100g self-raising flour

75g plain flour

125g butter

175g caster sugar

zest of 2 lemons

2 free-range eggs (50g), beaten

40ml milk

40g icing sugar, sifted

40ml lemon juice

TOPPING

50g very soft butter

100g icing sugar, sifted

150g Philadelphia cream cheese

zest of 2 lemons

12 gold balls

Preheat the oven to 180°C/350°F/gas 4 and put 12 paper cases into a muffin tray. Sieve the flours into a bowl.

Cream the butter, sugar and lemon zest in a bowl, using a hand-held electric whisk (or in a free-standing mixer using the whisk attachment), until pale. Scrape down the bowl while whisking. Once the mixture is pale, slowly add the beaten eggs a little at a time while continuing to whisk. Once the eggs have been incorporated, fold in the flour and milk with a large metal spoon – use the 'figure of eight' action – keeping air in the mix until you have an even colour (do not over-mix). The mixture should be of dropping consistency. Spoon the mixture into the paper cases, filling them three-quarters full, and bake in the preheated oven for 15–20 minutes, checking at 12 minutes. They should have risen and the top should feel springy. A wooden skewer stabbed into the sponge should come out clean.

While the cupcakes are cooking, mix the icing sugar with the lemon juice. To make the filling, cream the butter and icing sugar together and add the cream cheese and lemon zest. Mix until the filling is smooth, but take care not to over-beat or it will become runny.

When the cupcakes are ready, take them out of the oven. Leave them to rest in the tray for 5 minutes, then stab the top of the cakes with a wooden skewer. While the cakes are still warm, drizzle the top of each one with the lemon juice and icing mix. Leave them to cool. Pipe a swirl of the cream cheese topping over each cupcake and finish with a gold ball.

SPICED PEAR CUPCAKE

+ Makes 12 cupcakes   + Prep 35 minutes   + Cook 20 minutes   + Decorate 15 minutes

We have two pear trees in our garden that yield so much fruit we can't use it all, even in the bakery, so I have to keep coming up with more recipes for them. Pears and almonds work really well together, and I have come up with an almond topping that complements the pear beautifully in this autumnal cupcake.

First peel, halve and core the pears. Place 100g of the caster sugar in a heavy-bottomed pan with 100ml of water and heat until the sugar has dissolved. Add the star anise, vanilla pod and cinnamon stick and bring to the boil. Add the pear halves and poach until they are tender. Remove the pears from the syrup and chop into small pieces. Remove the vanilla pod and scrape out the vanilla seeds from the pod. Discard the pod and return the seeds to the poaching liquid. Set aside.

Preheat the oven to 180°C/350°F/gas 4 and put 12 paper cases into a muffin tray. Sieve the flour into a bowl.

Cream the butter with the remaining sugar and the vanilla in a bowl, using a hand-held electric whisk (or in a free-standing mixer using the whisk attachment), until pale. Scrape down the bowl while whisking. Once the mixture is pale, slowly add the beaten eggs a little at a time while continuing to whisk. Once the eggs have been incorporated, fold in the flour, chopped pears and milk with a large metal spoon – use the 'figure of eight' action – keeping air in the mix until you have an even colour (do not over mix). The mixture should be of dropping consistency. Spoon the mixture into the paper cases, filling them three-quarters full, and bake in the preheated oven for 15–20 minutes, checking at 12 minutes. They should have risen and the top should feel springy. A wooden skewer stabbed into the sponge should come out clean.

While the cupcakes are cooking, you can make the topping. Cream the butter and icing sugar together and add the cream cheese, ground almonds and vanilla. Mix until the topping is smooth, but take care not to over-beat or it will become runny.

Take the cupcakes out of the oven. Leave them to rest in the tray for 5 minutes, then drizzle them with the pear poaching liquid. Leave them to cool, then pipe a swirl of the almond topping on to each cupcake and finish with a few flaked almonds.

SPONGE

3 pears
275g caster sugar
1 star anise
1 vanilla pod
1 cinnamon stick
175g self-raising flour
125g butter
2 free-range eggs (50g), beaten
1 teaspoon good-quality vanilla extract or essence
40ml milk

TOPPING

50g very soft butter
120g icing sugar, sifted
100g Philadelphia cream cheese
50g ground almonds
1 teaspoon good-quality vanilla extract or essence
flaked almonds

COURGETTE CUPCAKE

+ Makes 10 cupcakes + Prep 15 minutes + Cook 20 minutes

Courgettes are such simple yet satisfying things to grow. We must have the smallest vegetable patch in the world, but just one plant yields so much. The kids get so excited when the courgettes develop into huge marrows – however, once you start making these little cupcakes your courgettes will all get used up and won't have the chance to get that big. This recipe uses the same technique as a carrot cake – the wet and dry ingredients are measured separately, then mixed together. These cakes are so moist, all they need is a simple dusting with icing sugar.

SPONGE

175g self-raising flour

½ level teaspoon ground cinnamon

½ level teaspoon grated nutmeg

1 level teaspoon bicarbonate of soda

150g soft light brown sugar

280g courgettes, grated

2 free-range eggs (50g), beaten

160ml sunflower oil

1 teaspoon good-quality vanilla extract or essence

TOPPING

icing sugar, sifted

Preheat the oven to 180°C/350°F/gas 4 and put 10 paper cases into a muffin tray. Sieve the flour, cinnamon, nutmeg and bicarbonate of soda into a bowl and stir in the sugar. Stir in the grated courgettes. In a second bowl beat the eggs and add the oil and vanilla. Fold the wet ingredients into the dry ingredients with a large metal spoon – use the 'figure of eight' action – keeping air in the mix until you have an even colour (do not over-mix). The mixture should be of dropping consistency. Spoon the mixture into the paper cases, filling them three-quarters full, and bake in the preheated oven for 15–20 minutes, checking at 12 minutes. The cupcakes should have risen and the top should feel springy. A wooden skewer stabbed into the sponge should come out clean.

Take the cupcakes out of the oven and leave them to cool in the tray. Dust them with icing sugar before serving.

ELDERFLOWER CUPCAKE

Makes 12 cupcakes + Prep 15 minutes + Cook 20 minutes + Decorate 10 minutes

I love elderflower cordial, so I thought I'd try to come up with a cupcake recipe for when elderflowers are in season. It's delicious as part of a summer picnic or as a snack after school sports day, with a chilled glass of elderflower cordial mixed with fizzy water and sprigs of mint.

Preheat the oven to 180°C/350°F/gas 4 and put 12 paper cases into a muffin tray. Sieve the flour into a bowl. Break up the elderflowers into little florets.

Cream the butter and sugar in a bowl, using a hand-held electric whisk (or in a free-standing mixer using the whisk attachment), until pale. Scrape down the bowl while whisking. Once the mixture is pale, slowly add the beaten eggs a little at a time while continuing to whisk. Once the eggs have been incorporated, fold in the flour and milk with a large metal spoon – use the 'figure of eight' action – keeping air in the mix until you have an even colour (do not over-mix). Stir in the elderflowers or elderflower cordial. The mixture should be of dropping consistency. Spoon the mixture into the paper cases, filling them halfway up, and bake in the preheated oven for 15–20 minutes, checking the cupcakes at 12 minutes. They should have risen and the top should feel springy. A wooden skewer stabbed into the sponge should come out clean.

While the cupcakes are cooking, you can start to make the topping. Cream the butter and icing sugar together, then add the cream cheese, the elderflower cordial and the food colour paste. Mix until the filling is smooth, but take care not to over-beat or it will become runny.

When the cupcakes are ready, take them out of the oven and leave them to cool in the tray. Spread them with the elderflower cream cheese topping.

SPONGE

175g self-raising flour

50g elderflowers or 2 teaspoons elderflower cordial, or both for a more intense flavour

125g butter

175g caster sugar

2 free-range eggs (50g), beaten

40ml milk

TOPPING

50g very soft butter

100g icing sugar, sifted

150g Philadelphia cream cheese

1 teaspoon elderflower cordial

2–3mm mint green food colour paste

RHUBARB FOOL CUPCAKE

+Makes 12 cupcakes   +Prep 40 minutes   +Cook 50 minutes

I love rhubarb fool. My mother's best friend, Stella, gave me a bunch of rhubarb from her garden last time I saw her, so I came up with this cupcake idea. It looks lovely with streaks of yellow custard, white whipped cream and the dark pink rhubarb purée spooned over the top – a great summer cupcake that can be eaten as a pudding.

SPONGE

175g self-raising flour
125g butter
175g caster sugar
1 teaspoon good-quality vanilla extract or essence
2 free-range eggs (50g), beaten

For the rhubarb purée
600g fresh rhubarb
150g caster sugar

TOPPING

300ml double cream
rhubarb purée (see above)

For the custard
4 egg yolks
20g caster sugar
½ level teaspoon cornflour
1 teaspoon good-quality vanilla extract or essence
300ml double cream

Place the rhubarb in a heavy-bottomed saucepan with the sugar and stew for 30 minutes over a low heat, stirring occasionally. You won't need to add any water, since the rhubarb gives off so much liquid. Set aside to cool.

Next make the custard. Mix the egg yolks, sugar, cornflour and vanilla together in a bowl large enough to take the cream as well. Heat the cream in a heavy-bottomed pan to just about boiling point, but do not let it actually boil. Pour the cream slowly over the egg paste in the bowl, stirring all the time. Strain the mixture back into the pan you used to heat the cream in and bring the custard up to just about boiling point, stirring all the time until it thickens, but do not let it boil. The custard needs to be quite thick for this topping. Set aside to cool.

Preheat the oven to 180°C/350°F/gas 4 and put 12 paper cases into a muffin tray. Sieve the flour into a bowl.

Cream the butter, sugar and vanilla in a bowl, using a hand-held electric whisk (or in a free-standing mixer using the whisk attachment), until pale. Scrape down the bowl while whisking. Once the mixture is pale, slowly add the beaten eggs a little at a time while continuing to whisk. Once the eggs have been incorporated, fold in the flour with a large metal spoon – use the 'figure of eight' action – keeping air in the mix until you have an even colour (do not over-mix). The mixture should be of dropping consistency. Add a little milk if necessary, then fold in 60g of the cold rhubarb purée. Spoon the mixture into the paper cases, filling them three-quarters full, and bake for 15–20 minutes, checking at 12 minutes. They should have risen and the top should feel springy. A wooden skewer stabbed into the sponge should come out clean.

While the cupcakes are cooking, you can finish the custard and topping. Whip the cream for the custard until it holds soft peaks, and fold it into the custard so you have streaks of white and yellow. Whip the cream for the topping.

Take the cupcakes out of the oven and leave them to cool in the tray. Spoon some whipped cream and custard on to each cupcake and add as much rhubarb purée as you like – I like lots, so it pours down the sides.

ROSE AND PISTACHIO CUPCAKE

+Makes 12 cupcakes   +Prep 15 minutes   +Cook 20 minutes   +Decorate 10 minutes

This cupcake is so pretty, with its rosewater sponge studded with bright green pistachio nuts topped with a pastel rose icing and chopped pistachios. The pink and green look great together and are reminiscent of a Middle Eastern banquet. Perfect after a spicy lamb tagine.

Preheat the oven to 180°C/350°F/gas 4 and put 12 paper cases into a muffin tray. Sieve the flour into a bowl.

Cream the butter, sugar and vanilla in a bowl, using a hand-held electric whisk (or in a free-standing mixer using the whisk attachment), until pale. Scrape down the bowl while whisking. Once the mixture is pale, slowly add the beaten eggs a little at a time while continuing to whisk. Once the eggs have been incorporated, fold in the flour, milk and rosewater with a large metal spoon – use the 'figure of eight' action – keeping air in the mix until you have an even colour (do not over-mix). The mixture should be of dropping consistency. Stir in the toasted pistachios.

Spoon the mixture into the paper cases, filling them halfway up, and bake in the preheated oven for 16–20 minutes, checking the cupcakes at 12 minutes. They should have risen and the top should feel springy. A wooden skewer stabbed into the sponge should come out clean.

While the sponges are cooking, you can start to make the topping. Cream the butter and icing sugar together, then add the cream cheese and rosewater. Mix until the filling is smooth, but take care not to over-beat or it will become runny. Add the pink colour paste, a little at a time, on the end of a spoon.

When the cupcakes are ready, take them out of the oven and leave them to cool in the tray. Fill a piping bag with the vanilla cream cheese topping and pipe swirls over the top of each cupcake. Finish with finely chopped pistachios.

SPONGE

175g self-raising flour

125g butter

175g caster sugar

1 teaspoon good-quality vanilla extract or essence

2 free-range eggs (50g), beaten

20ml milk

20ml rosewater

40g lightly toasted pistachio nuts, chopped

TOPPING

50g very soft butter

100g icing sugar, sifted

150g Philadelphia cream cheese

2 teaspoons rosewater

2–3mm pink food colour paste

40g pistachio nuts, chopped

SAVOURY WHOOPIES AND CUPCAKES

I just couldn't resist the chance to try out some recipes for savoury whoopies and cupcakes. I think they all work really well as canapés, because they're very small, with a burst of flavour. Most of the fillings and toppings in this chapter have been served at parties over the years by my catering business, which I've been running for twenty years now. They are really easy to make, and you can mix and match them as you like or simply use them as dips. The whoopie and cupcake sponges can also be served as a snack with drinks.

WHOOPIES

CUPCAKES

GRUYÈRE AND CARAMELIZED ONION WHOOPIE

+ Makes 60–70 whoopies (2–3 cm across)   + Prep 25 minutes   + Cook 6 minutes

I've been making a caramelized onion and Gruyère tart for years – in fact, one of my clients likes them so much they order them in different sizes: mini for canapés, medium for a finger food party and large for a buffet. This is my whoopie take on it. The technique for this particular whoopie is so simple – you just weigh out the wet ingredients, then the dry ingredients, and mix them together before baking.

SPONGE

190g plain flour

½ level teaspoon bicarbonate of soda

½ level teaspoon salt

½ level teaspoon pepper

70ml buttermilk

100g butter, melted

1 free-range egg (50g), beaten

60g onions, finely chopped

100g Gruyère cheese, grated

FILLING

20g butter

200g onions, finely chopped

2 teaspoons soft light brown sugar

salt and freshly ground black pepper

100g Gruyère cheese, grated

TOPPING

Gruyère cheese, grated

sea salt

Preheat the oven to 200°C/400°F/gas 6 and line a baking tray with grease-proof paper. Sieve the flour, bicarbonate of soda, salt and pepper into a bowl. Mix the buttermilk with the melted butter and beaten egg.

Mix the wet ingredients into the dry ingredients with a large metal spoon – use the 'figure of eight' action – keeping air in the mix until you have an even colour (do not over-mix). Stir in the onions and Gruyère. Pipe or use a teaspoon to spoon 2cm dollops (at least 2cm high) on to the baking tray, spacing them well apart to allow for spreading, and bake in the preheated oven for 6 minutes.

While the sponges are cooking you can start to make the filling. Melt the butter in a pan, add the onions and fry gently until softened. Add the sugar, salt and pepper and continue frying until the onions become a caramel colour. Take off the heat and tip them into a clean bowl. Mix in the Gruyère while the onions are still hot. Taste and add more salt and pepper if necessary.

Take the sponges out of the oven and leave to cool on the tray. When cool, lift them off with a fish slice. Sandwich them together with the Gruyère and caramelized onion filling and sprinkle the top with grated Gruyère and a little sea salt.

Before serving, preheat the oven to 200°C/400°F/gas 6. Pop the whoopies in for 5 minutes, and serve warm.

PARMESAN AND CAYENNE WHOOPIE

+ Makes 60–70 whoopies (2–3 cm across) + Prep 25 minutes + Cook 2 hours

This is a great canapé to serve if you have a few friends over for drinks. The combination of Parmesan and cayenne really complements the goat's cheese and basil, and the slow-roasted cherry tomato topping looks very pretty. I have made a lighter base here by using whisked egg whites in the sponge. By mixing the wet and dry ingredients separately, then folding in the whisked egg whites, you get lovely light savoury whoopies.

First roast the cherry tomatoes for the topping. Preheat the oven to 150°C/350°F/gas 4. Halve the tomatoes and arrange them on a baking tray. Sprinkle with the balsamic vinegar, dried basil, salt and pepper and roast in the preheated oven for 2 hours.

When you are ready to make the whoopies, preheat the oven to 200°C/400°F/gas 6 and line a baking tray with greaseproof paper. Sieve the flour, mustard, cayenne, salt and pepper into a bowl. Mix the melted butter with the beaten egg.

Mix the wet ingredients into the dry ingredients and stir in the Parmesan. Whisk the egg whites in a bowl and fold them into the whoopie mix with a large metal spoon – use the 'figure of eight' action – keeping air in the mix until you have an even colour (do not over-mix). Pipe or use a teaspoon to spoon 2cm dollops (at least 2cm high) on to the baking tray, spacing them well apart to allow for spreading, and bake in the preheated oven for 6 minutes.

While the sponges are cooking, you can start to make the filling. Mash the goat's cheese with the milk by hand or in a blender. Add the chopped basil leaves and season with salt and pepper.

Take the sponges out of the oven and leave to cool on the tray. When cool, lift them off with a fish slice. Sandwich them together with the goat's cheese cream, reserving some for the top. Pipe a small blob of goat's cheese cream in the centre of each whoopie, and add a roasted cherry tomato half and a little leaf of basil.

SPONGE

180g plain flour

2 level teaspoons mustard powder

½ level teaspoon cayenne pepper

½ level teaspoon salt

½ level teaspoon freshly ground black pepper

75g butter, melted

1 free-range egg (50g), beaten

3 free-range egg whites (50g)

100g Parmesan cheese

FILLING

100g goat's cheese

50ml milk

10 fresh basil leaves, chopped

salt and freshly ground white pepper

TOPPING

8 cherry tomatoes

2 tablespoons balsamic vinegar

½ level teaspoon dried basil

salt and freshly ground white pepper

60–70 small fresh basil leaves

SPINACH AND GRUYÈRE WHOOPIE

+ Makes 60–70 whoopies (2–3 cm across) + Prep 25 minutes + Cook 6 minutes

I make a large number of spinach and Gruyère breakfast canapés at work, and the same combination works really well as a whoopie. You don't have to be veggie to enjoy this one.

SPONGE

180g plain flour

½ level teaspoon bicarbonate of soda

½ level teaspoon salt

½ level teaspoon freshly ground black pepper

150g butter, melted

1 free-range egg (50g), beaten

100g fresh spinach, finely chopped

3 free-range egg whites (50g)

100g Gruyère cheese

FILLING

25g butter

30g plain flour

150ml milk

20ml double cream

salt and freshly ground black pepper

grated nutmeg

100g fresh spinach, chopped

100g Gruyère cheese

Preheat the oven to 200°C/400°F/gas 6 and line a baking tray with grease-proof paper. Sieve the flour, bicarbonate of soda, salt and pepper into a bowl. Mix the melted butter with the beaten egg.

Mix the wet ingredients into the dry ingredients and stir in the finely chopped spinach. Whisk the egg whites in a bowl and fold them into the whoopie mix with a large metal spoon – use the 'figure of eight' action – keeping air in the mix until you have an even colour (do not over-mix). Pipe or use a teaspoon to spoon 2cm dollops (at least 2cm high) on to the baking tray, spacing them well apart to allow for spreading, and bake in the preheated oven for 6 minutes.

While the sponges are cooking, you can start to make the filling. Melt the butter in a saucepan. Add the flour and stir until you have a paste. Gradually add the milk and bring to the boil, stirring all the time, until you have a thick sauce. If it becomes lumpy, take the pan off the heat and stir or whisk vigorously. Add the cream, salt, pepper and nutmeg, then stir in the spinach and Gruyère. You need the sauce to be quite thick. Taste and add more salt and pepper if necessary.

Take the sponges out of the oven and leave to cool on the tray. When cool, lift them off with a fish slice. Sandwich them together with the spinach sauce and serve warm or at room temperature.

SUN-DRIED TOMATO AND BASIL WHOOPIE
+ Makes 60–70 whoopies (2–3 cm across) + Prep 25 minutes + Cook 20 minutes

A very strong-tasting whoopie – these flavours are right up my street! If you don't fancy having a go at roasting the red pepper yourself, you can buy a jar of roasted peppers from the supermarket. Likewise, instead of making the bean purée you can use a ready-made baba ganoush (aubergine purée) or hummus.

First roast the red peppers for the filling. Either hold the peppers directly over a gas flame, or bake them in a preheated oven at 240°C/475°F/gas 9 for 15–20 minutes until the skin is blackened. Place the peppers in a plastic bag or in a bowl covered in clingfilm until they are cool enough to handle. The skin should now come away easily. Halve the peppers and clean out the seeds, then slice the flesh into strips.

Preheat the oven to 200°C/400°F/gas 6 and line a baking tray with grease-proof paper. Sieve the flour, bicarbonate of soda, salt and pepper into a bowl. Mix the milk with the melted butter and beaten egg.

Mix the wet ingredients into the dry ingredients and stir in the sun-dried tomatoes and chopped basil. Whisk the egg whites in a bowl and fold them into the whoopie mix with a large metal spoon – use the 'figure of eight' action – keeping air in the mix until you have an even colour (do not over-mix). Pipe or use a teaspoon to spoon 2cm dollops (at least 2cm high) on to the baking tray, spacing them well apart to allow for spreading, and bake in the preheated oven for 6 minutes.

While the sponges are cooking, you can start to make the bean purée filling. Put the beans and crushed garlic into a blender and blend for 20 seconds. Add the olive oil and season with salt and pepper. If the mixture is too thick, add more oil. I tend to hold back on the olive oil because I don't like the purée too oily.

Take the sponges out of the oven and leave to cool on the tray. When cool, lift them off with a fish slice. Sandwich them together with the bean purée and a few strips of roasted red pepper.

SPONGE
150g plain flour

½ level teaspoon bicarbonate of soda

½ level teaspoon salt

½ level teaspoon freshly ground black pepper

30g milk

80g butter, melted

1 free-range egg (50g), beaten

40g sun-dried tomatoes in oil, drained and chopped

a bunch of fresh basil, chopped

3 free-range egg whites (50g)

FILLING
For the roasted pepper

2 large red peppers

For the bean purée

1 x 400g tin of flageolet, haricot or cannellini beans, drained and rinsed

2 cloves of garlic, crushed

50ml olive oil

salt and freshly ground black pepper

OLIVE AND ROSEMARY WHOOPIE

+ Makes 60–70 whoopies (2–3 cm across) + Prep 25 minutes + Cook 6 minutes

Olives and rosemary work really well together. At the bakery, we make delicious bread with this flavour combination and I thought it would work well for a Mediterranean whoopie canapé. I have filled this one with an olive tapenade, but you could use a cream cheese filling. Alternatively you could use a little dolcelatte cheese, a few rocket leaves and a thin slice of tomato to make a whoopie sandwich!

SPONGE

180g plain flour

½ level teaspoon
bicarbonate of soda

½ level teaspoon salt

½ level teaspoon freshly
ground black pepper

75g butter, melted

1 free-range egg (50g),
beaten

50g Parmesan cheese

50g pitted black olives,
chopped

leaves from 2 sprigs
of rosemary

3 free-range egg whites
(50g)

FILLING

100g pitted olives

4 anchovy fillets, drained

50g fresh parsley

20g capers, rinsed

1 level teaspoon
Dijon mustard

olive oil

freshly ground black pepper

Preheat the oven to 200°C/400°F/gas 6 and line a baking tray with grease-proof paper. Sieve the flour, bicarbonate of soda, salt and pepper into a bowl. Mix the melted butter with the beaten egg.

Mix the wet ingredients into the dry ingredients and stir in the Parmesan, chopped black olives and rosemary leaves. Whisk the egg whites in a bowl and fold them into the whoopie mix with a large metal spoon – use the 'figure of eight' action – keeping air in the mix until you have an even colour (do not over-mix). Pipe or use a teaspoon to spoon 2cm dollops (at least 2cm high) on to the baking tray, spacing them well apart to allow for spreading, and bake in the preheated oven for 6 minutes.

While the sponges are cooking, you can start to make the filling. Place the olives, anchovies, parsley, capers and mustard in a food processor and blend until smooth. Add some olive oil to loosen the mix if it is too stiff, and season with pepper. The mix will be salty enough because of the anchovies.

Take the sponges out of the oven and leave to cool on the tray. When cool, lift them off with a fish slice and sandwich them together with the tapenade filling.

PORCINI WHOOPIE

+ Makes 60–70 whoopies (2–3 cm across)   + Prep 25 minutes   + Cook 6 minutes

Maybe it's my Polish heritage, but I love mushrooms! In this whoopie I have combined a sponge containing dried porcini with a rich mushroom and garlic filling.

Preheat the oven to 200°C/400°F/gas 6 and line a baking tray with grease-proof paper. Place the dried porcini in a bowl and pour over 50ml of boiling water. Leave for 5 minutes, then squeeze out the water and chop the porcini finely. Sieve the flour, bicarbonate of soda, salt and pepper into a bowl. Mix the melted butter with the beaten egg.

Mix the wet ingredients into the dry ingredients and stir in the chopped porcini. Whisk the egg whites in a bowl and fold them into the whoopie mix with a large metal spoon – use the 'figure of eight' action – keeping air in the mix until you have an even colour (do not over-mix). Pipe or use a teaspoon to spoon 2cm dollops (at least 2cm high) on to the baking tray, spacing them well apart to allow for spreading, and bake in the preheated oven for 6 minutes.

While the sponges are cooking you can start to make the filling. Finely chop the button mushrooms (if you have a blender you can do this in seconds). Melt the butter in a saucepan and add the onion and garlic. Cook for 5 minutes, until the onion and garlic are soft. Add the mushrooms and cook until all their liquid has cooked out and you have a thick paste. Add a little cream to loosen the mixture to a spreadable consistency, then season with salt, pepper and thyme.

Take the sponges out of the oven and leave to cool on the tray. When cool, lift them off with a fish slice and sandwich together with the mushroom filling.

SPONGE

20g dried porcini
   mushrooms

180g plain flour

½ level teaspoon
   bicarbonate of soda

½ level teaspoon salt

½ level teaspoon freshly
   ground black pepper

150g butter, melted

1 free-range egg (50g),
   beaten

3 free-range egg whites
   (50g)

FILLING

250g button mushrooms

20g butter

¼ of an onion, chopped

1 clove of garlic, crushed

20ml double cream

salt and freshly ground
   black pepper

leaves from 2 sprigs
   of fresh thyme

CROQUE MONSIEUR WHOOPIE

+Makes 60–70 whoopies (2–3 cm across) +Prep 25 minutes +Cook 6 minutes

Ham and cheese are such a great combination, and this French classic is a favourite at every event I cater for.

SPONGE

180g plain flour

½ level teaspoon bicarbonate of soda

½ level teaspoon salt

½ level teaspoon freshly ground black pepper

75g butter, melted

1 free-range egg (50g), beaten

100g Gruyère cheese, finely grated

3 free-range egg whites (50g)

FILLING

25g butter

30g plain flour

150ml milk

20ml double cream

salt and freshly ground black pepper

grated nutmeg

100g Gruyère cheese, grated

cherry tomato slices

8 slices of smoked ham

Preheat the oven to 200°C/400°F/gas 6 and line a baking tray with grease-proof paper. Sieve the flour, bicarbonate of soda, salt and pepper into a bowl. Mix the melted butter with the beaten egg.

Mix the wet ingredients into the dry ingredients and stir in the Gruyère. Whisk the egg whites in a bowl and fold them into the whoopie mix with a large metal spoon – use the 'figure of eight' action – keeping air in the mix until you have an even colour (do not over-mix). Pipe or use a teaspoon to spoon cm dollops (at least 2cm high) on to the baking tray, spacing them well apart to allow for spreading, and bake in the preheated oven for 6 minutes.

While the sponges are cooking, you can start to make the filling. Melt the butter in a saucepan. Add the flour and stir until you have a paste. Gradually add the milk and bring to the boil, stirring all the time, until you have a thick sauce. If it becomes lumpy, take the pan off the heat and stir or whisk vigorously. Add the cream, salt, pepper and nutmeg, then the grated Gruyère. You need the sauce to be quite thick. Using a pastry cutter, cut the ham into little rounds, one for each whoopie.

Take the sponges out of the oven and leave to cool on the tray. When cool, lift them off with a fish slice. Sandwich them together with the rounds of ham and most of the Gruyère béchamel. Pipe or spoon a small blob of béchamel in the centre of each whoopie, and add a little extra Gruyère and a cherry tomato slice.

Before serving, preheat the oven to 200°C/400°F/gas 6. Pop the whoopies in for 5 minutes, and serve warm.

CHEDDAR WHOOPIE WITH A LEEK AND MUSTARD BÉCHAMEL

+ Makes 60–70 whoopies (2–3 cm across)   + Prep 25 minutes   + Cook 11 minutes

This is one for my best friend, Anne. She lives in Australia now but is originally from Wales, and she always buys me the most fantastic cookery books when she is over for a visit.

Preheat the oven to 200°C/400°F/gas 6 and line a baking tray with grease-proof paper. Sieve the flour, salt and pepper into a bowl and make a well in the centre. Mix the melted butter with the beaten egg.

Mix the wet ingredients into the dry ingredients and stir in the grated Cheddar and spring onions. Whisk the egg whites in a bowl and fold them into the whoopie mix with a large metal spoon – use the 'figure of eight' action – keeping air in the mix until you have an even colour (do not over-mix). Pipe or use a teaspoon to spoon 2cm dollops (at least 2cm high) on to the baking tray, spacing them well apart to allow for spreading, and bake in the preheated oven for 6 minutes.

While the sponges are cooking you can start to make the filling. Melt half the butter in a frying pan and soften the leeks over a low heat for 10 minutes. Don't let the leeks burn, or they will taste bitter. Melt the rest of the butter in a pan. Add the flour and stir until you have a paste. Gradually add the milk and bring to the boil, stirring all the time, until you have a thick sauce. If it becomes lumpy, take the pan off the heat and stir or whisk vigorously. Add the cream, salt, pepper and mustard powder, then stir in the grated Cheddar and the leeks. You need the sauce to be quite thick.

Take the sponges out of the oven and leave to cool on the tray. When cool, lift them off with a fish slice and sandwich together with the leek and mustard béchamel.

Before serving, preheat the oven to 200°C/400°F/gas 6. Pop the whoopies in for 5 minutes, and serve warm.

SPONGE

180g plain flour

1 level teaspoon bicarbonate of soda

½ level teaspoon salt

½ level teaspoon freshly ground black pepper

100g butter, melted

1 free-range egg (50g), beaten

3 free-range egg whites (50g)

100g Cheddar cheese, finely grated

50g spring onions, finely chopped

FILLING

50g butter

200g leeks, chopped

30g plain flour

150ml milk

20ml double cream

salt and freshly ground black pepper

1 level teaspoon English mustard powder

100g Cheddar cheese, grated

RYE WHOOPIE WITH SMOKED SALMON, CREAM CHEESE AND CHIVES

+ Makes 60–70 whoopies (2–3 cm across) + Prep 25 minutes + Cook 6 minutes

Rye and salmon is a favourite Swedish combination. I have filled this whoopie with softened cream cheese and chives, and topped it with a curl of smoked salmon. Enjoy it with a chilled glass of bubbly – very civilized!

SPONGE
50g plain flour

50g dark rye flour

50g light rye flour

½ level teaspoon salt

½ level teaspoon freshly ground black pepper

½ level teaspoon bicarbonate of soda

150g butter, melted

1 free-range egg (50g), beaten

3 free-range egg whites (50g)

FILLING
200g cream cheese

a small bunch of chives, finely chopped

juice of ½ a lemon

salt and freshly ground black pepper

TOPPING
100g smoked salmon

juice of ½ a lemon

a bunch of chives, chopped

Preheat the oven to 200°C/400°F/gas 6 and line a baking tray with grease-proof paper. Sieve the flours, salt, pepper and bicarbonate of soda into a bowl. Mix the melted butter with the beaten egg.

Mix the wet ingredients into the dry ingredients. Whisk the egg whites in a bowl and fold them into the whoopie mix with a large metal spoon – use the 'figure of eight' action – keeping air in the mix until you have an even colour (do not over-mix). Pipe or use a teaspoon to spoon 2cm dollops (at least 2cm high) on to the baking tray, spacing them well apart to allow for spreading, and bake in the preheated oven for 6 minutes.

While the sponges are cooking, you can start to make the filling. Mix the cream cheese, chives and lemon juice and season with salt and pepper. For the topping, make curls of smoked salmon by twisting 10 x 3cm strips around your finger.

Take the sponges out of the oven and leave to cool on the tray. When cool, lift them off with a fish slice and sandwich them together with the cream cheese filling, reserving some for the top. Pipe a swirl of the filling over each whoopie, and finish with a curl of smoked salmon. Just before serving, squeeze a little lemon juice over the salmon and add a few chopped chives and a sprinkle of pepper.

CORN AND CHILLI CUPCAKE

+ Makes 24–30 mini cupcakes + Prep 20 minutes + Cook 10 minutes

This little bright yellow corn cake is flecked with red chilli and topped with green guacamole, soured cream and Cheddar cheese. It looks so pretty, and is a real Mexican taste explosion. Great with a really dry chilled white wine or a frozen Margarita on a hot summer's evening.

Preheat the oven to 180°C/350°F/gas 4 and put 24–30 mini paper cases on a baking tray. Sieve the flour, bicarbonate of soda and salt into a bowl and stir in the polenta. Mix the buttermilk with the beaten eggs, sunflower oil and chilli.

Mix the wet ingredients into the dry ingredients with a large metal spoon – use the 'figure of eight' action – keeping air in the mix until you have an even colour (do not over-mix). The mixture should be of dropping consistency. Spoon the mixture into the paper cases, filling them three-quarters full, and bake in the preheated oven for 10 minutes.

While the cupcakes are cooking, you can start to make the guacamole for the filling. Cut the tomato into small cubes (I don't mind the seeds, so I don't scoop them out). Finely chop the onion, chilli and coriander. Mash the avocado and mix it with half the lemon juice to stop it discolouring. Stir in the chopped tomato, onion, chilli, coriander, salt and pepper. Mix well and taste it – surprisingly it needs quite a lot of salt.

When the cupcakes are ready, take them out of the oven and leave them to cool on the tray. Top each one with a heaped teaspoon of guacamole filling and ½ a teaspoon of soured cream. Finish with a little grated Cheddar and, if you want to be fancy, a leaf of coriander.

SPONGE

75g plain flour

1 level teaspoon bicarbonate of soda

1 level teaspoon salt

200g polenta

100ml buttermilk

2 free-range eggs (50g), beaten

100ml sunflower oil

1 fresh red chilli, finely chopped

TOPPING

50g soured cream

50g mature Cheddar cheese, grated

24–30 fresh coriander leaves (optional)

For the guacamole

1 tomato

½ a red onion

1 jalapeño or other green chilli

a large bunch of fresh coriander

1 avocado

juice of 2 lemons

1 teaspoon salt

1 teaspoon freshly ground black pepper

RYE CUPCAKE TOPPED WITH SMOKED TROUT MOUSSE

+Makes 24–30 mini cupcakes +Prep 15 minutes +Cook 10 minutes

SPONGE

100g dark rye flour

100g light rye flour

75g plain flour

½ level teaspoon bicarbonate of soda

½ level teaspoon salt

100ml milk

100g butter, melted

2 free-range eggs (50g), beaten

a large bunch of fresh dill

TOPPING

cayenne pepper

a small bunch of fresh dill

For the trout mousse

150g smoked trout

50g Philadelphia cream cheese

25g mayonnaise

25ml double cream

2 spring onions, finely chopped

juice of 1 lemon

1 level teaspoon salt

1 level teaspoon freshly ground black pepper

My dad is an obsessive fisherman. When I was little he would take me fishing with him at every opportunity. Camping by a reservoir and getting up at dawn with the birds, it was really fun. I wasn't too bad at the fishing, but he was excellent and we had so many trout we didn't know what to do with them. We used to smoke them in the back garden in an old fish kettle and then make this delicious smoked trout mousse (my mother's recipe).

Preheat the oven to 180°C/350°F/gas 4 and put 24–30 mini paper cases on to a baking tray. Sieve the flour, bicarbonate of soda and salt into a bowl. Mix the milk with the melted butter and beaten eggs.

Mix the wet ingredients into the dry ingredients with a large metal spoon – use the 'figure of eight' action – keeping air in the mix until you have an even colour (do not over-mix). The mixture should be of dropping consistency. Spoon the mixture into the paper cases, filling them three-quarters full, and bake in the preheated oven for 10 minutes.

While the cupcakes are cooking, you can start to make the smoked trout mousse for the topping. Put all the ingredients into a blender or mash them together in a bowl. If the mix is a bit thick, add a little more mayonnaise or double cream.

When the cupcakes are ready, take them out of the oven and leave them to cool on the tray. Pipe or spoon a 3 cm dollop of the smoked trout mousse on top of each cooled cupcake, sprinkle with cayenne and top with a little frond of dill.

PARMESAN AND ROSEMARY CUPCAKE WITH PESTO CREAM AND SUN-DRIED TOMATO

Makes 24–30 mini cupcakes + Prep 15 minutes + Cook 10 minutes

This is a light, cheesy cupcake topped with pesto cream cheese. I have included my recipe for pesto here, but you can, of course, use a ready-made pesto from the supermarket if you don't have time to make your own. The recipe makes more pesto than you will need, but it is difficult to make a smaller amount and it keeps well in the fridge.

Preheat the oven to 180°C/350°F/gas 4 and put 24–30 mini paper cases on to a baking tray. Sieve the flour, bicarbonate of soda, Parmesan and salt into a bowl. Stir in the rosemary leaves. Mix the milk with the melted butter and beaten eggs.

Mix the wet ingredients into the dry ingredients with a large metal spoon – use the 'figure of eight' action – keeping air in the mix until you have an even colour (do not over-mix). The mixture should be of dropping consistency. Spoon the mixture into the paper cases, filling them three-quarters full, and bake in the preheated oven for 10 minutes.

While the sponges are cooking, you can start to make the topping. Put all the ingredients for the pesto into a blender and whiz until smooth. Put the cream cheese into a bowl, add 50g of the pesto and mix until you have a smooth, bright green paste. Put the rest of the pesto into the fridge for another day.

When the cupcakes are ready, take them out of the oven and leave them to cool on the tray. Pipe some of the pesto cream cheese over each cupcake and top with a piece of sun-dried tomato.

SPONGE

200g plain flour

1 level teaspoon bicarbonate of soda

75g Parmesan cheese, grated

½ level teaspoon salt

2 sprigs of fresh rosemary, leaves picked and finely chopped

100ml milk

100ml butter, melted

2 free-range eggs (50g), beaten

TOPPING

24–30 small pieces of sun-dried tomato

For the pesto

50g fresh basil leaves

20g pinenuts

50g Parmesan cheese, grated

salt and freshly ground black pepper

10ml extra virgin olive oil

For the pesto cream cheese

100g Philadelphia cream cheese

50g pesto, homemade or bought

FETA, SPINACH AND DILL CUPCAKE

+ Makes 24–30 mini cupcakes   + Prep 15 minutes   + Cook 10 minutes

This mini savoury cupcake is delicious served warm or cool for a picnic. You don't need to add any salt to the recipe because the feta is already salty. In place of dill, try using oregano or marjoram.

SPONGE

200g plain flour

1 level teaspoon
  bicarbonate of soda

salt and freshly ground
  black pepper

1 level teaspoon
  garlic powder

100ml buttermilk

2 free-range eggs (50g),
  beaten

100ml sunflower oil

100g feta cheese, crumbled

100g fresh spinach,
  chopped

a small bunch of fresh dill

Preheat the oven to 180°C/350°F/gas 4 and put 24–30 mini paper cases on to a baking tray. Sieve the flour, bicarbonate of soda, salt and garlic powder into a bowl. Mix the buttermilk with the beaten egg and sunflower oil and add the crumbled feta, spinach and dill.

Mix the wet ingredients into the dry ingredients with a large metal spoon – use the 'figure of eight' action – keeping air in the mix until you have an even colour (do not over-mix). The mixture should be of dropping consistency. Spoon the mixture into the paper cases, filling them three-quarters full, and bake in the preheated oven for 10 minutes.

When the cupcakes are ready, take them out of the oven. They are delicious eaten while still warm, but if you are making them to eat later, let them cool down on the tray. Before serving, preheat the oven to 150°C/300°F/gas 3 and pop the cupcakes in for 5 minutes to reheat.

SMOKED PANCETTA CUPCAKE TOPPED WITH PURPLE SPROUTING BROCCOLI

+ Makes 24–30 mini cupcakes + Prep 25 minutes + Cook 20 minutes

I got this idea from watching Jamie Oliver make an Italian soup. He roasted smoked pancetta and anchovies, then layered them with cavolo nero before pouring stock over the top. I thought a dry version would work really well as a bruschetta topping, and I have been serving it as a pre-dinner party snack for the last couple of summers. Here, I have taken it a step further and topped a delicious corn cupcake with this salty, crisp vegetable. Fantastic!

First fry the smoked pancetta cubes in a little olive oil until crispy (watch that they don't burn) and set aside to cool.

Blanch the broccoli for the topping in a saucepan of boiling water. Refresh in cold water and chop into pieces small enough to fit on top of the cupcakes. Place the broccoli on a baking tray and add the anchovies and the oil from their tin. Bake in the preheated oven for 10 minutes, until the anchovies have dissolved. Remove from the oven and set aside.

Preheat the oven to 180°C/350°F/gas 4 and put 24–30 mini paper cases on to a baking tray. Sieve the flour, polenta, bicarbonate of soda and salt into a bowl and make a well in the centre. Mix the buttermilk with the beaten eggs and sunflower oil and add the basil and the fried pancetta. Mix the wet ingredients into the dry ingredients with a large metal spoon – use the 'figure of eight' action – keeping air in the mix until you have an even colour (do not over-mix). The mixture should be of dropping consistency. Spoon the mixture into the paper cases, filling them three-quarters full, and bake in the preheated oven for 10 minutes.

While the cupcakes are cooking, fry the smoked pancetta strips in a little sunflower oil until crispy and break into pieces.

When the cupcakes are ready, take them out of the oven and leave them to cool on the tray. Top them with a little of the purple sprouting broccoli mix and finish with a piece of smoked pancetta, placed at an angle. Serve warm.

SPONGE

100g smoked pancetta, cut into cubes

175g plain flour

50g polenta

1 level teaspoon bicarbonate of soda

½ level teaspoon salt

50ml buttermilk

2 free-range eggs (50g), beaten

100ml sunflower oil

a small bunch of fresh basil, chopped

TOPPING

200g purple sprouting broccoli

1 small tin of anchovies, including the oil

100g smoked pancetta strips, thinly sliced

sunflower oil

WACKY WHOOPIES AND CUPCAKES

The wacky whoopies and cupcakes in this chapter look fiddly, but honestly, they are really not difficult. I am no artist, but because the whoopies are small, decorating them is less daunting than decorating a big cake. Remain calm, plan ahead, and in no time at all you'll have beautiful cakes with loads of wow factor.

For some of these wacky whoopies I have used roll-out icing, water icing, or a mixture of the two, together with sweets. The great thing is that whoopies are so versatile – once you start thinking of ideas you can't stop. I have made suggestions for colours and sweets, but you can use whatever you have in your cupboard. Use cake-boards or a tray to place your finished wacky whoopies on, and once you have got your confidence you can start decorating the boards as well, by covering the surface with an appropriate butter icing to complement your whoopie. Draw a web for the hairy spider, for example, or put the caterpillar on green grass

If you can, try to make the sponges the day before, so that they are slightly firmer than usual and easier to work with. The icing colours and fillings can also be made the day before – the colours keep really well for up to three days. If you have done all the prep the night before it will leave you with nothing to do but create away on the day!

WHOOPIES

CUPCAKES

FRIENDLY DINOSAUR WHOOPIE

+Makes 4 dinosaurs +Prep 25 minutes +Cook 8 minutes +Decorate 1½ hours

A large whoopie covered in roll-out icing, with shaped sponges for the head and tail, makes a great dinosaur. You will have some offcuts of sponge left over, but I am sure you will find someone to eat them. If you like, you can make bigger dinosaurs by spooning out larger dollops of mixture. I have suggested an orange dinosaur with brown spikes, but you can play around with the colours – greens, browns and dark pinks all work really well.

Preheat the oven to 200°C/400°F/gas 6 and line 2 baking trays with grease-proof paper. Sieve the flour and bicarbonate of soda into a bowl. Mix the buttermilk with the vanilla and orange food colour paste and set aside.

Cream the butter and sugar together in a bowl, using a hand-held electric whisk (or in a free standing mixer using the whisk attachment), until pale. Scrape down the bowl while whisking. Once the mixture is pale, slowly add the beaten egg a little at a time while continuing to whisk. Once the egg has been incorporated, fold in the wet and dry ingredients with a large metal spoon – use the 'figure of eight' action – keeping air in the mix until you have an even colour (do not over-mix). Pipe or spoon 12 x 4cm dollops (at least 4cm high) on to one of the baking trays and 8 x 3cm dollops (at least 3cm high) on to the other one, spacing them well apart to allow for spreading. Bake the larger sponges for 8 minutes and the smaller ones for 7 minutes.

For the filling, cream the butter and icing sugar together and add the cream cheese and vanilla. Mix until smooth, but take care not to over-beat or it will become runny. Add the orange food colour paste a little at a time.

Take 20g of the white roll-out icing and set aside for the eyes. Divide the rest of the roll-out icing into 320g and 140g balls. Colour the 320g ball with the orange colour paste by kneading the paste into the icing until you have your desired depth of colour. Repeat, using the brown food colour paste for the 140g ball.

To make the black water icing, sift the icing sugar into a bowl and add the water, a little at a time, stirring until you have quite a thick paste but one that is loose enough to pipe or spoon on to the whoopies. Add the black food colour paste a little at a time, on the end of a spoon. Take the sponges out of the oven and leave to cool on the tray. When cool, lift them off with a fish slice.

To assemble each dinosaur, sandwich 2 large sponges together with some of the orange cream cheese filling to make the dinosaur's body. Sandwich 2 small sponges for the dinosaur's head. Halve another large sponge. Out of one half cut a small semi-circle near the edge and shape a tail with a point at the end. Fix the head and tail in place with the orange cream cheese filling. Paint more filling over the whole dinosaur shape. Divide the orange roll-out icing into 4 equal balls. Roll one of them out to a 22 x 12cm oval, then, lifting it carefully, wrap the dinosaur. Roll out the reserved white icing and make 2 circles for the eyes.

Divide the brown roll-out icing into 4 equal balls. Take one of the balls and shape 9 cone shapes for the dinosaur spikes and 4 small balls for the feet. Place 3 spikes down the body, 2 on the tail, 3 across the top of the head and 1 as a horn/nose on the face. Squash the small balls with your finger to make feet and mark toes with a fork. Fix them on to the body. Fill a piping bag with the black water icing and pipe on eyebrows, black dots on the eyes and nostrils and a smiley mouth. There you have your friendly dinosaur!

SPONGE

180g plain flour

1 level teaspoon bicarbonate of soda

90g buttermilk

1 teaspoon good quality vanilla extract or essence

1 teaspoon orange food colour paste

80g butter

140g caster sugar

1 free-range egg (50g), beaten

FILLING

75g very soft butter

150g icing sugar, sifted

225g Philadelphia cream cheese

1½ teaspoon good-quality vanilla extract or essence

1 teaspoon orange food colour paste

TOPPING

For the orange and brown roll-out icing

480g white roll-out icing

3–5mm orange and brown food colour paste

For the black water icing

70g icing sugar.

1 tablespoon water

3–5mm black food colour paste

CATERPILLAR WHOOPIE
+ Makes an 8-whoopie caterpillar + Prep 25 minutes + Cook 8 minutes + Decorate 1 hour

The inspiration for this cute birthday cake came from my little boy's love of the story *The Very Hungry Caterpillar*. It looks so pretty, and is sure to be devoured immediately. You will need a red velvet whoopie for the head, so I usually make up a batch (see page 26) and eat the rest! I tend to use 8 whoopies to make the body, but you can use as many as you like. If you want a stronger green, add more colouring.

SPONGE
180g plain flour

1 level teaspoon bicarbonate of soda

90ml buttermilk

1 teaspoon good-quality vanilla extract or essence

½ teaspoon green food colour paste

80g butter

140g caster sugar

1 free-range egg (50g), beaten

FILLING
50g very soft butter

100g icing sugar, sifted

150g Philadelphia cream cheese

1 teaspoon good-quality vanilla extract or essence

2–3mm each of yellow and red food colour paste

Preheat the oven to 200°C/400°F/gas 6 and line a baking tray with grease-proof paper. Sieve the flour and bicarbonate of soda into a bowl. Mix the buttermilk with the vanilla and green food colour paste and set aside.

Cream the butter and sugar together in a bowl, using a hand-held electric whisk (or in a free-standing mixer using the whisk attachment), until pale. Scrape down the bowl while whisking. Once the mixture is pale, slowly add the beaten egg a little at a time while continuing to whisk. Once the egg has been incorporated, fold in the wet and dry ingredients with a large metal spoon – use the 'figure of eight' action – keeping air in the mix until you have an even colour (do not over-mix). Pipe or spoon 16 x 4cm dollops (at least 4cm high) on to the baking tray, spacing them well apart to allow for spreading, and bake in the preheated oven for 8 minutes.

While the sponges are cooking, you can start to make the filling and topping. For the filling, cream the butter and icing sugar together, then add the cream cheese and vanilla. Mix until the filling is smooth, but take care not to over-beat or it will become runny. Remove a tablespoon of the filling to a cup and add the red colour paste, a little at a time, on the end of a spoon. Add the yellow colour paste to the remaining filling mixture in the same way.

To make the water icing for the topping, sift the icing sugar into a bowl and add the water, a little at a time, stirring until you have quite a thick paste but one that is loose enough to pipe or spoon on to the whoopies. Divide the icing between 4 bowls and colour each batch with one of the 4 colour pastes – red, yellow, black and green.

When the sponges are ready, take them out of the oven and leave them to cool on the tray. When cool, lift them off with a fish slice.

To assemble your caterpillar, sandwich the green sponges together with the yellow filling. Sandwich the red velvet sponges with the red filling. Pipe the green water icing on top of the green whoopies and set aside to dry for 5 minutes.

Pipe black and yellow water icing stripes on to the green whoopies. Pipe the red water icing on top of the red velvet whoopie and position two yellow Smarties for the eyes while the icing is still wet. When dry, pipe a smile on to the face. Position the body and head of the caterpillar on a cake-board so they are slightly overlapping (as in the photo). They can be stuck into position using a little green water icing.

Cut 2 short bits from the red or black laces and stick on to the caterpillar's head to make the antennae. Cut 6 short legs from the red or black laces and stick them into the last whoopie and the third and fourth whoopie.

There. Now you have your own Very Hungry Caterpillar!

Colour your board/tray with any leftover green icing to make it look like grass, or make some green butter icing if you have time.

TOPPING

2 yellow Smarties

4 fizzy strawberry or black liquorice laces

2 red velvet sponges (see page 26)

For the water icing

420g icing sugar

6 tablespoons water

2–3mm each of red, yellow, black and green food colour paste

LIZARD HEAD WHOOPIE

+Makes 8 lizard heads +Prep 20 minutes +Cook 8 minutes +Decorate 25 minutes

My friend Rebecca, who lives in New York, told me about this one – she made it for her little boy's birthday party. One green whoopie with a green water icing topping, liquorice allsort eyes and a long red tongue. It's really easy.

SPONGE

180g plain flour

1 level teaspoon
bicarbonate of soda

90ml buttermilk

1 teaspoon good-quality
vanilla extract or essence

1 teaspoon bright
green food colour paste

80g butter

140g caster sugar

1 free-range egg (50g),
beaten

FILLING

50g very soft butter

100g icing sugar, sifted

150g Philadelphia
cream cheese

1 teaspoon good-quality
vanilla extract or essence

4–5mm green
food colour paste

TOPPING

16 yellow liquorice allsorts

8 fizzy strawberry
or rainbow laces

For the green water icing

280g icing sugar

4 tablespoons water

4–5mm green food
colour paste

Preheat the oven to 200°C/400°F/gas 6 and line a baking tray with grease-proof paper. Sieve the flour and bicarbonate of soda into a bowl. Mix the buttermilk with the vanilla and green food colour paste and set aside.

Cream the butter and sugar together in a bowl, using a hand-held electric whisk (or in a free-standing mixer using the whisk attachment), until pale. Scrape down the bowl while whisking. Once the mixture is pale, slowly add the beaten egg a little at a time while continuing to whisk. Once the egg has been incorporated, fold in the wet and dry ingredients with a large metal spoon – use the 'figure of eight' action – keeping air in the mix until you have an even colour (do not over-mix). Pipe or spoon 16 x 4cm dollops (at least 4cm high) on to the baking tray, spacing them well apart to allow for spreading, and bake in the preheated oven for 8 minutes.

While the sponges are cooking you can start to make the filling and topping. For the filling, cream the butter and icing sugar together and add the cream cheese and vanilla. Mix until the filling is smooth, but take care not to over-beat or it will become runny. Add the green food colour paste, a little at a time, on the end of a spoon.

For the green water icing, sift the icing sugar into a bowl and add the water, a little at a time, stirring until you have quite a thick paste but one that is loose enough to pipe or spoon on to the whoopies. Add the green food colour paste, a little at a time, on the end of a spoon.

Take the sponges out of the oven and leave to cool on the tray. When cool, lift them off with a fish slice.

To assemble each lizard head, sandwich 2 green sponges together with the green cream cheese icing. Pipe the green water icing on top of your whoopie and pop the liquorice allsort eyes on before the icing dries (if you put the eyes on later the icing will crack). Curl the tip of a strawberry or rainbow lace and fix it in place with some water icing. Place it in the lizard's mouth.

FROG PRINCE WHOOPIE

+ Makes 16 frogs   + Prep 20 minutes   + Cook 8 minutes   + Decorate 1 hour

This is another easy one, using royal purple sponges cut in half and covered in roll-out icing. You simply stand the semicircular halves on their flat edges, give them purple bulbous eyes and webbed feet, and you have a pond full of princes!

SPONGE

135g plain flour

1 level teaspoon
  bicarbonate of soda

50ml buttermilk

1 teaspoon good-quality
  vanilla extract or essence

1 teaspoon bright purple
  food colour paste

60g butter

100g caster sugar

1 free-range egg (50g),
  beaten

*see page 164 for Filling
  and Topping*

Preheat the oven to 200°C/400°F/gas 6 and line a baking tray with greaseproof paper. Sieve the flour and bicarbonate of soda into a bowl. Mix the buttermilk with the vanilla and purple food colouring and set aside.

Cream the butter and sugar together in a bowl, using a hand-held electric whisk (or in a free-standing mixer using the whisk attachment), until pale. Scrape down the bowl while whisking. Once the mixture is pale, slowly add the beaten egg a little at a time while continuing to whisk. Once the egg has been incorporated, fold in the wet and dry ingredients with a large metal spoon – use the 'figure of eight' action – keeping air in the mix until you have an even colour (do not over-mix). Pipe or spoon 16 x 4cm dollops (at least 4cm high) on to the baking tray, spacing them well apart to allow for spreading, and bake in the preheated oven for 8 minutes.

While the sponges are cooking, you can start to make the filling and topping. Cream the butter and icing sugar together and add the cream cheese and vanilla. Mix until the filling is smooth, but take care not to over-beat or it will become runny. Add the purple food colour paste, a little at a time, on the end of a spoon.

Take the sponges out of the oven and leave to cool on the tray. When cool, lift them off with a fish slice.

To make the water icing for the topping, sift the icing sugar into a bowl and add the water, a little at a time, stirring until you have quite a thick paste but one that is loose enough to pipe or spoon on to the whoopies. Divide the water icing between 2 bowls, and colour one purple, the other black.

continued on page 164

FILLING

65g very soft butter

130g icing sugar, sifted

200g Philadelphia
cream cheese

1 teaspoon good-quality
vanilla extract or essence

4–5mm purple
food colour paste

TOPPING

For the purple roll-out icing

960g white roll-out icing

4–5mm purple
food colour paste

For the black water icing

70g icing sugar

1 tablespoon water

4–5mm black
food colour paste

Cut off 20g of the white roll-out icing and set aside. Colour the remaining icing with the purple colour paste by kneading the paste into the icing until you have your desired depth of colour.

To assemble each frog prince, sandwich 2 sponges together with the purple classic cream cheese filling. Cut the whoopies in half, then spread some more purple cream cheese filling over the whoopie halves and stand them up on their flat edge to make the body of the frog. Repeat with the rest of the sponges.

Cut off 320g of the purple roll-out icing and set this aside. Divide the rest of the icing into 16 balls. Dust your work surface with icing sugar and roll one ball out to make a 14 x 11cm oval. Lifting the oval carefully, drape it over the body of the frog. Repeat to cover the rest of the frogs.

From some of the reserved purple icing, make the frog's bulbous eyes. Attach a little of the reserved white roll-out icing to the front of each eye with black water icing and place on either side of the curve, fixing in place with a very small amount of black water icing. With your black water icing, pipe on a pupil and give him a smile.

Shape the rest of the purple icing into 2 webbed feet and mark webs with a fork. Place the feet at the front of the frog's semicircular body and fix them in place with black water icing. He's finished. Get the kids to make paper crowns and crown them their frog princes!

OCTOPUS WHOOPIE

+ Makes 7 octopuses   + Prep 20 minutes   + Cook 6 minutes   + Decorate 1½ hours

The inspiration for this whoopie came from *Toy Story 3*. You can make him in lots of different colours, but I've chosen red and blue. Three little red velvet sponges are draped in coloured roll-out icing and given eight curled legs. For a little girl you can make a red or pink octopus, while for a boy a blue, purple or green one would work really well. It is so easy to make.

Preheat the oven to 200°C/400°F/gas 6 and line a baking tray with grease-proof paper. Sieve the flour, cocoa powder and bicarbonate of soda into a bowl. Mix the buttermilk with the vanilla and red food colouring and set aside.

Cream the butter and sugar together in a bowl, using a hand-held electric whisk (or in a free-standing mixer using the whisk attachment), until pale. Scrape down the bowl while whisking. Once the mixture is

pale, slowly add the beaten egg a little at a time while continuing to whisk. Once the egg has been incorporated, fold in the wet and dry ingredients with a large metal spoon – use the 'figure of eight' action – keeping air in the mix until you have an even colour (do not over-mix). Pipe or spoon 21 x 2cm dollops (at least 2cm high) on to the baking tray, spacing them well apart to allow for spreading, and bake in the preheated oven for 5–6 minutes.

While the sponges are cooking, you can start to make the filling and topping. For the filling, cream the butter and icing sugar together and add the cream cheese and vanilla. Mix until the filling is smooth, but take care not to over-beat or it will become runny. Add the blue colour paste, a little at a time, on the end of a spoon.

To make the water icing, sift the icing sugar into a bowl and add the water, a little at a time, stirring until you have quite a thick paste but one that is loose enough to pipe or spoon on to the whoopies. Divide the water icing between 2 bowls. Colour one blue and one black, adding the colour paste a little at a time, on the end of a spoon.

Cut off 20g of the white roll-out icing and set aside for the eyes. Colour the remaining icing with the blue colour paste by kneading the paste into the icing until you have your desired depth of colour.

Take the sponges out of the oven and leave to cool on the tray. When cool, lift them off with a fish slice.

To assemble each octopus, sandwich 2 sponges with the cream cheese filling and fix a third sponge on top to make the body. Coat the whole shape with more cream cheese filling. Divide the blue roll-out icing into 7 equal balls. Take one ball and divide it in half. Roll one half out into a 15cm diameter circle, then, lifting the circle of icing carefully, drape it over the body and fix it underneath. Add the leftover scraps to the other half of the ball, then divide it into 8 for the legs and roll out into long sausages. Fix them under the octopus with a little of your blue water icing. Position the legs so that they curve on to your board (see the photo).

Take a small amount from the reserved white roll-out icing to make eyes for your octopus and place them in position. Fill a piping bag with the black water icing and pipe on pupils and a mouth.

All done!

SPONGE

90g plain flour

2 level teaspoons cocoa powder

1 level teaspoon bicarbonate of soda

30ml buttermilk

1 teaspoon good-quality vanilla extract or essence

2 teaspoons red liquid food colouring (Dr Oetker)

40g butter

75g brown sugar

1 free-range egg (50g), beaten

FILLING

50g very soft butter

100g icing sugar, sifted

150g Philadelphia cream cheese

1 teaspoon good-quality vanilla extract or essence

2cm blue colour paste

TOPPING

For the blue and black water icing

70g icing sugar

1 tablespoon water

4–5mm each of blue and black food colour paste

For the blue roll-out icing

545g white roll-out icing

4–5mm blue food colour paste

HAIRY SPIDER WHOOPIE

+Makes 5 spiders   +Prep 20 minutes   +Cook 8 minutes   +Decorate 1 hour

SPONGE

140g plain flour

40g cocoa powder

1 level teaspoon
  bicarbonate of soda

90ml buttermilk

1 teaspoon good-quality
  vanilla extract or essence

80g butter

140g soft light brown sugar

1 free-range egg (50g),
  beaten

FILLING

35g very soft butter

75g icing sugar, sifted

100g Philadelphia
  cream cheese

1 teaspoon good-quality
  vanilla extract or essence

2cm black food colour
  paste

TOPPING

liquorice twists

10 yellow Jelly Tots

100g dark chocolate
  vermicelli

100g light chocolate
  vermicelli

*For the chocolate
  butter icing*

100g very soft butter

125g icing sugar, sifted

20g cocoa powder

This whoopie is brilliant for little boys! The recipe uses the basic chocolate sponge, and I have filled the whoopies with a black vanilla cream cheese filling so that when you take a bite the spider will ooze black blood. It is then coated in butter icing and decorated with dark and light brown vermicelli to give it a hairy look. The kids will love it.

Preheat the oven to 200°C/400°F/gas 6 and line a baking tray with grease-proof paper. Sieve the flour, cocoa powder and bicarbonate of soda into a bowl. Mix the buttermilk with the vanilla and set aside.

Cream the butter and sugar together in a bowl, using a hand-held electric whisk (or in a free-standing mixer using the whisk attachment), until pale. Scrape down the bowl while whisking. Once the mixture is pale, slowly add the beaten egg a little at a time while continuing to whisk. Once the egg has been incorporated, fold in the wet and dry ingredients with a large metal spoon – use the 'figure of eight' action – keeping air in the mix until you have an even colour (do not over-mix). Pipe or spoon 8 x 4cm dollops (at least 4cm high) on to one of the baking trays, and 8 x 3cm dollops (at least 3cm high) on to the other, spacing them well apart to allow for spreading. Bake the large ones in the preheated oven for 8 minutes and the small ones for 5 minutes.

For the filling, cream the butter and icing sugar together, then add the cream cheese and vanilla. Mix until the filling is smooth, but take care not to over-beat or it will become runny. Add the black colour paste, a little at a time, on the end of a spoon. To make the chocolate butter icing for the topping, cream the butter, icing sugar and cocoa powder together and beat until smooth.

Take the sponges out of the oven and leave to cool on the tray. When cool, lift them off with a fish slice.

To assemble each spider, sandwich 2 large sponges and 2 small sponges together with the black cream cheese filling. The big whoopie is the spider's body and the small whoopie is his head. Stick the head and body together with chocolate butter icing, and use the rest to coat the whole spider.

Mix the vermicelli together and sprinkle over the body and head. Push 2 pieces of liquorice into the head for the antennae and 4 liquorice pieces into each side of the body for the legs. Finish with 2 yellow Jelly Tot eyes.

HEDGEHOG WHOOPIE

+ Makes 7 hedgehogs   + Prep 20 minutes   + Cook 8 minutes   + Decorate 1 hour

I saw an article in my local paper about a hedgehog that had broken three legs and had been fitted with splints – he was 'a bit wonky but doing well'. He looked so sweet being held in someone's hand. I thought he would make a great whoopie – he does, and he's not at all wonky!

Preheat the oven to 200°C/400°F/gas 6 and line a baking tray with grease-proof paper. Sieve the flour, cocoa powder and bicarbonate of soda into a bowl. Mix the buttermilk with the vanilla and set aside.

Cream the butter and sugar together in a bowl, using a hand-held electric whisk (or in a free-standing mixer using the whisk attachment), until pale. Scrape down the bowl while whisking. Once the mixture is pale, slowly add the beaten egg a little at a time while continuing to whisk. Once the egg has been incorporated, fold in the wet and dry ingredients with a large metal spoon – use the 'figure of eight' action – keeping air in the mix until you have an even colour (do not over-mix). Pipe or spoon 16 x 4cm dollops (at least 4cm high) on to the baking tray, spacing them well apart to allow for spreading, and bake in the preheated oven for 8 minutes.

For the filling, cream the butter, cocoa powder and icing sugar together and beat until smooth. To make the white water icing, sift the icing sugar into a bowl and add the water, a little at a time, stirring until you have quite a thick paste but one that is loose enough to pipe or spoon on to the whoopies. Colour the white roll-out icing with the black food colour paste by kneading the paste into the icing until you have your desired depth of colour.

To assemble each hedgehog, sandwich 2 sponges together with the chocolate butter filling. Then cut one sponge into quarters and push one quarter between the body halves for the head. Fix the head and body together with chocolate butter filling, then coat the whole hedgehog.

Cut each Mikado biscuit into 3 pieces and stick them into the hedgehog's body to look like spikes. Push 2 chocolate buttons into the head to make ears.

Divide the black roll-out icing into 7 equal parts. Take 1 piece and roll into a sausage shape. Take out 2 equal ½cm balls for the eyes and a 1cm piece for the nose. Divide the rest into 4 to make the feet, and mark with a fork. Place into positions. Repeat for all the hedgehogs.

SPONGE

140g plain flour

40g cocoa powder

1 level teaspoon bicarbonate of soda

90ml buttermilk

1 teaspoon good-quality vanilla extract or essence

80g butter

140g soft light brown sugar

1 free-range egg (50g), beaten

FILLING

150g very soft butter

20g cocoa powder

250g icing sugar, sifted

TOPPING

14 chocolate buttons

7x 39g packets of Mikado biscuits or Matchmakers

For the white water icing

70g icing sugar

1 tablespoon water

For the black roll-out icing

250g white roll-out icing

4–5mm black food colour paste

BEEHIVE WHOOPIE

+Makes 3 beehives +Prep 20 minutes +Cook 8 minutes +Decorate 1 hour

This is for my lovely friend Mel, who lives in New Zealand. She is obsessed with manuka honey and believes it is the cure for everything. I think this whoopie looks really cute, and if it doesn't cure everything it will certainly make you smile. I have included a honey sponge recipe for those of you who love manuka honey as much as Mel!

SPONGE

100g plain flour

1 level teaspoon
bicarbonate of soda

2 teaspoons buttermilk

1 teaspoon good-quality
vanilla extract or essence

40g butter

40g caster sugar

1 free-range egg (50g),
beaten

1 level teaspoon manuka
honey (or other runny
honey)

FILLING

150g very soft butter

280g icing sugar, sifted

3–5mm yellow food colour
paste

TOPPING

9 white chocolate buttons

9 cocktail sticks

*For the yellow and black
roll-out icing*

90g white roll out icing

3–5mm yellow food
colour paste

3–5mm black food
colour paste

For the white water icing

70g icing sugar

1 tablespoon water

Preheat the oven to 200°C/400°F/gas 6 and line 3 baking trays with grease-proof paper. Sieve the flour and bicarbonate of soda into a bowl. Mix the buttermilk with the vanilla and set aside.

Cream the butter and sugar together in a bowl, using a hand-held electric whisk (or in a free-standing mixer using the whisk attachment), until pale. Scrape down the bowl while whisking. Once the mixture is pale, slowly add the beaten egg a little at a time while continuing to whisk. Once the egg has been incorporated, fold in the wet and dry ingredients with a large metal spoon – use the 'figure of eight' action – keeping air in the mix until you have an even colour (do not over-mix). Pipe or spoon 6 x 4cm dollops (at least 4cm high) on to one of the baking trays, spacing them well apart to allow for spreading. On a second tray pipe or spoon 6 x 3cm dollops (at least 3cm high) in the same way, and on a third tray pipe or spoon 6 x 2cm dollops (at least 2cm high). Bake the small sponges in the preheated oven for 5 minutes, the medium ones for 7 minutes and the large ones for 8 minutes.

While the sponges are cooking, you can start to make the filling and topping. Cream the butter and icing sugar together and beat until the filling is smooth, but take care not to over-beat or it will become runny. Add the yellow food colour paste, a little at a time, on the end of a spoon.

Colour half the white roll-out icing with the yellow food colour paste by kneading the paste into the icing until you have your desired depth of colour. Repeat, using the black food colour paste for the rest. For the white water icing, sift the icing sugar into a bowl and add the water, a little at a time, stirring until you have quite a thick paste but one that is loose enough to pipe or spoon on to the whoopies.

Take the sponges out of the oven and leave to cool on the trays. When cool, lift them off with a fish slice. To assemble each beehive, sandwich a large, a medium and a small sponge one on top of the other with the yellow butter filling. Pipe more icing over the pile of sponges in a circular motion, to get the effect of a hive. Roll out the yellow roll-out icing into a long sausage and cut into 18 discs. Repeat with the black roll-out icing, then sandwich two yellow and two black discs alternately together to give you a bee.

Pipe on 2 dots of the white water icing for the eyes. Add a smile and leave to dry. Cut the white chocolate buttons in half and fix 2 halves on each bee's back to look like wings. Attach the bees to cocktail sticks and add 3 bees to the top of each hive.

FAIRY PRINCESS WHOOPIE

+ Makes 4 princesses   + Prep 20 minutes   + Cook 8 minutes   + Decorate 1 hour

One for the girls! Although I only have little boys, I have a lovely collection of god-daughters, so I can appreciate the importance of pink. The eldest is seventeen and the youngest nine months, but they all loved these whoopies, although poor Edie (the nine-month-old) could only look. It's a strawberry sponge skirt of different shades of pink icing (using a number 7 star piping nozzle), decorated with pink sprinkles, around a ballerina doll. Definitely pretty in pink.

SPONGE

100g plain flour

1 level teaspoon bicarbonate of soda

20ml strawberry purée

1 teaspoon red food colour paste

40g butter

75g caster sugar

1 free-range egg (50g), beaten

FILLING

320g very soft butter

640g icing sugar, sifted

2–3mm pink food colour paste

TOPPING

4 small (about 10cm high) dolls

thin pink ribbon

glitter sparkles

For the pink water icing

140g icing sugar

2 tablespoons water

2–3mm pale pink food colour paste

Preheat the oven to 200°C/400°F/gas 6 and line a baking tray with grease-proof paper. Sieve the flour and bicarbonate of soda into a bowl. Mix the strawberry purée with the red food colour paste and set aside.

Cream the butter and sugar together in a bowl, using a hand-held electric whisk (or in a free-standing mixer using the whisk attachment), until pale. Scrape down the bowl while whisking. Once the mixture is pale, slowly add the beaten egg a little at a time while continuing to whisk. Once the egg has been incorporated, fold in the dry ingredients and the strawberry mixture with a large metal spoon – use the 'figure of eight' action – keeping air in the mix until you have an even colour (do not over-mix). Pipe or spoon 8 x 4cm dollops (at least 4cm high) on to the baking tray, spacing them well apart to allow for spreading, and bake in the preheated oven for 8 minutes.

While the sponges are cooking, you can start to make the filling and topping. For the filling, cream the butter and icing sugar together and beat until smooth. Add the colour paste a little at a time, on the end of a spoon. For the topping, sift the icing sugar into a bowl and add the water, a little at a time, stirring until you have quite a thick paste but one that is loose enough to pipe or spoon on to the whoopies. Add the colour paste, a little at a time, on the end of a spoon.

Take the sponges out of the oven and leave to cool on the tray. When cool, lift them off with a fish slice.

To assemble each princess, sandwich 2 sponges together with the pink butter icing filling. Then cut the whoopie from the centre to the edge, so you can place the sponge around the doll like a skirt. Pipe or spread the pale pink water icing around the body to make the top of the skirt. Then coat the rest in butter icing. Pipe on butter-icing stars with a number 7 star piping nozzle, tie a ribbon around your princess's waist, and sprinkle her dress with glitter.

FLOWER HEAD WHOOPIE

+ Makes 2 flower heads + Prep 20 minutes + Cook 8 minutes + Decorate 30 minutes

A collection of coloured whoopies, all with yellow centres and brightly coloured petals – I suggest red, purple or pink. If you want to make the petals and stamens different sizes you can play around with some pastry cutters and have some fun making a pretty garden.

Preheat the oven to 200°C/400°F/gas 6 and line 2 baking trays with grease-proof paper. Sieve the flour and bicarbonate of soda into a bowl. Mix the buttermilk with the vanilla and set aside.

Cream the butter and sugar together in a bowl, using a hand-held electric whisk (or in a free standing mixer using the whisk attachment), until pale. Scrape down the bowl while whisking. Once the mixture is pale, slowly add the beaten egg a little at a time while continuing to whisk. Once the egg has been incorporated, fold in the wet and dry ingredients with a large metal spoon – use the 'figure of eight' action – keeping air in the mix until you have an even colour (do not over-mix). Pipe or spoon 20 x 3cm dollops (at least 3cm high) on to one of the baking trays, spacing them well apart to allow for spreading. On a second baking tray pipe or spoon 4 x 2 cm dollops (at least 2cm high). Bake the large ones in the preheated oven for 7 minutes and the small ones for 5 minutes.

While the sponges are cooking, you can start to make the filling and topping. For the filling, cream the butter and icing sugar together and add the cream cheese and vanilla. Mix until the filling is smooth, but take care not to over-beat or it will become runny. Take out 20g of the filling and colour it yellow, adding the food colour paste on the end of a spoon. Then colour the rest the same way with your chosen petal colour.

For the topping, sift the icing sugar into a bowl and add the water, a little at a time, stirring until you have quite a thick paste but one that is loose enough to pipe or spoon on to the whoopies. Add the colour paste, a little at a time, on the end of a spoon.

Take the sponges out of the oven and leave to cool on the tray. When cool, lift them off with a fish slice.

To assemble each flower head, sandwich the sponges together with your chosen cream cheese filling colours. Top with your choice of coloured water icing. Place the yellow in the centre and the petals around the edge and you have a very pretty flower.

SPONGE

200g plain flour

1 level teaspoon bicarbonate of soda

50ml buttermilk

1 teaspoon good-quality vanilla extract or essence

80g butter

100g caster sugar

1 free-range egg (50g), beaten

FILLING

50g very soft butter

100g icing sugar, sifted

150g Philadelphia cream cheese

1 teaspoon good-quality vanilla extract or essence

a little yellow food colour paste

4–5mm food colour paste of your choice

TOPPING

140g icing sugar

2 tablespoons water

4–5mm food colour paste of your choice

BUTTERFLY CUPCAKE

+ Makes 9 butterflies + Prep 15 minutes + Cook 20 minutes + Decorate 1 hour

This is a lovely girly cupcake. Make sure the cupcake cases are quite full before baking, so that you get a dome on top of each cake when they're cooked.

SPONGE

175g self-raising flour

125g butter

175g caster sugar

1 teaspoon good-quality vanilla extract or essence

2 free-range eggs (50g), beaten

40ml milk

TOPPING

pink sprinkles or silver balls

fizzy strawberry laces

For the bright pink butter icing

100g very soft butter

200g icing sugar, sifted

1 teaspoon good-quality vanilla extract or essence

4–5mm pink food colour paste

For the pink and black water icing

140g icing sugar

2 tablespoon water

4–5mm each of pink and black food colour paste

Preheat the oven to 180°C/350°F/gas 4 and put 12 paper cases into a muffin tray. Sieve the flour into a bowl.

Cream the butter, sugar and vanilla in a bowl using a handheld electric whisk (or in a free-standing mixer using the whisk attachment), until pale. Scrape down the bowl while whisking. Once the mixture is pale, slowly add the beaten eggs a little at a time while continuing to whisk. Once the eggs have been incorporated, fold in the flour and milk with a large metal spoon – use the 'figure of eight' action – keeping air in the mix until you have an even colour (do not over-mix). The mixture should be of dropping consistency. Spoon the mixture into the paper cases, filling them nearly to the top, and bake in the preheated oven for 15–20 minutes, checking at 12 minutes. The cupcakes should have risen and the top should feel springy. A wooden skewer stabbed into the sponge should come out clean.

Cream the butter and icing sugar together and add the vanilla. Mix until the filling is smooth, but take care not to over-beat or it will become runny. Add the pink food colour paste, a little at a time, on the end of a spoon.

To make the pink and black water icing, sift the icing sugar into a bowl and add the water, a little at a time, stirring until you have quite a thick paste but one that is loose enough to pipe or spoon on to the cupcakes. Divide the mixture between 2 bowls and add the pink food colour paste to one and the black to the other, a little at a time, on the end of a spoon.

When the cupcakes are ready, take them out of the oven and leave them to cool in the tray. To make your butterfly cakes, cut the domed top off each cupcake and cut them in half. Ice the halves with pink water icing and decorate with sprinkles or silver balls. Set aside to dry.

Spread the pink butter icing over the top of each cupcake, reserving some icing for the body. Place the 2 halves of the dome at an angle on top of the cupcake to look like wings and fix them in place with pink butter icing, finishing with a blob for the head. Pipe a strip of pink water icing along the top of the butter icing. Cut 2 pieces from the laces and place either side of the head to make the antennae. With your black water icing, pipe 2 dots for the eyes.

ALIEN CUPCAKE
+ Makes 12 aliens + Prep 15 minutes + Cook 20 minutes + Decorate 45 minutes

The little alien in *Toy Story* was so cute that I just had to make a cupcake out of him. I have added some green colour paste to the vanilla mix for an extra alien feel. I have put in quantities for the eyes and ears, but you can choose to make them larger or smaller if you like. I have allowed a leeway with the amount of icing so you shouldn't run out.

SPONGE

175g self-raising flour

40ml milk

1 teaspoon green
food colour paste

125g butter

175g caster sugar

2 free-range eggs (50g),
beaten

1 teaspoon good-quality
vanilla extract or essence

Preheat the oven to 180°C/350°F/gas 4 and put 12 paper cases into a muffin tray. Sieve the flour into a bowl. Mix the milk with the green food colour paste and set aside.

Cream the butter, sugar and vanilla in a bowl, using a hand-held electric whisk (or in a free-standing mixer using the whisk attachment), until pale. Scrape down the bowl while whisking. Once the mixture is pale, slowly add the beaten eggs a little at a time while continuing to whisk. Once the eggs have been incorporated, fold in the flour and green milk with a large metal spoon – use the 'figure of eight' action – keeping air in the mix until you have an even colour (do not over-mix). The mixture should be of dropping consistency.

Spoon the mixture into the paper cases, filling them halfway up, and bake in the preheated oven for 15–20 minutes, checking at 12 minutes. The cupcakes should have risen and the top should feel springy. A wooden skewer stabbed into the sponge should come out clean.

While the cupcakes are cooking you can start to make the topping. For the green cream cheese topping, cream the butter and icing sugar together and add the cream cheese and vanilla. Mix until the filling is smooth, but take care not to over-beat or it will become runny. Add the green food colour paste, a little at a time, on the end of a spoon, and mix until you have a really bright green.

For the black water icing, sift the icing sugar into a bowl and add the water, a little at a time, stirring until you have quite a thick paste but one that is loose enough to pipe or spoon on to the whoopies. Add the black food colour paste, a little at a time, on the end of a spoon.

Set aside 30g of the white roll-out icing for the eyes. Colour the remaining icing with the green food colour paste by kneading the paste into the icing until you have your desired depth of colour.

When the cupcakes are ready, take them out of the oven and leave them to cool in the tray.

To assemble each alien, first divide the green roll-out icing into 12 balls, one for each cupcake. Take 3 small bits from one of these balls and fashion 2 of the bits into spiky ears and one into a spike for the antenna. Do the same with the other 11 balls and set these aside to firm up.

Spread the top of each cupcake with the green cream cheese topping. Dust a work surface with icing sugar, then roll out the reserved white roll-out icing into a long sausage and cut it into pieces to make the alien's bulbous eyes. Place them in a curve on the cupcake. Place the ears on either side and stick the antenna above the middle eye. Pipe a pupil of black water icing in the centre of the eye, and a little oval mouth.

TOPPING

For the green vanilla cream cheese topping
40g very soft butter
80g icing sugar, sifted
120g Philadelphia cream cheese
1 teaspoon good-quality vanilla extract or essence
4–5mm green food colour paste

For the black water icing
70g icing sugar, sifted
1 tablespoon water
4–5mm black food colour paste

For the green roll-out icing
120g white roll-out icing
green food colour paste

GINGER CAT CUPCAKE

+Makes 12 cupcakes   +Prep 15 minutes   +Cook 20 minutes   +Decorate 45 minutes

When our youngest son was born we bought him a cat as a present 'from the baby'. He is the most tolerant cat in the world. I have made this cupcake in his honour. He is ginger and deserves a medal for what he puts up with from my boys. Make your cat face any colour you like.

SPONGE

175g self-raising flour

125g butter

175g caster sugar

1 teaspoon good-quality vanilla extract or essence

2 free-range eggs (50g), beaten

40ml milk

Preheat the oven to 180°C/350°F/gas 4 and put 12 paper cases into a muffin tray. Sieve the flour into a bowl.

Cream the butter, sugar and vanilla in a bowl, using a hand-held electric whisk (or in a free-standing mixer using the whisk attachment), until pale. Scrape down the bowl while whisking. Once the mixture is pale, slowly add the beaten eggs a little at a time while continuing to whisk. Once the eggs have been incorporated, fold in the flour and milk with a large metal spoon – use the 'figure of eight' action – keeping air in the mix until you have an even colour (do not over-mix). The mixture should be of dropping consistency. Spoon the mixture into the paper cases, filling them halfway up, and bake in the preheated oven for 15–20 minutes, checking at 12 minutes. The cupcakes should have risen and the top should feel springy. A wooden skewer stabbed into the sponge should come out clean.

While the cupcakes are cooking, you can start to make the topping. For the orange butter icing, cream the butter and icing sugar together and add the vanilla. Mix until the filling is smooth, but take care not to over-beat or it will become runny. Add the orange colour paste, a little at a time, on the end of a spoon.

To make the black water icing, sift the icing sugar into a bowl and add the water, a little at a time, stirring until you have quite a thick paste but one that is loose enough to pipe or spoon on to the whoopies. Add the black food colour paste, a little at a time, on the end of a spoon. Colour the white roll-out icing with the orange food colour paste by kneading the paste into the icing until you have your desired depth of colour.

When the cupcakes are ready, take them out of the oven and leave them to cool in the tray.

To make your cat faces, first spread the orange butter icing over the top of each cupcake, reserving a little. Dust a work surface with icing sugar and roll out the orange roll-out icing. Cut out 24 cat's ears and fix them in place with some of the reserved butter icing. Put the Jelly Tot eyes in place.

Cut the strawberry laces into 2 short sticks for the nose and fix in place to make a T-shape. Stick strawberry or cola lace whiskers on either side of the T. With your black water icing, dot the eyes with pupils.

TOPPING

24 Jelly Tots

24 fizzy strawberry or cola laces

For the orange butter icing

100g very soft butter

200g icing sugar, sifted

1 teaspoon good-quality vanilla extract or essence

2–3mm orange food colour paste

For the black water icing

70g icing sugar

1 tablespoon water

4–5mm black food colour paste

For the orange roll-out icing

100g white roll-out icing

2–3mm orange food colour paste

CLOWN CUPCAKE

I Makes 12 cupcakes + Prep 15 minutes + Cook 20 minutes + Decorate 1 hour

These clown faces come complete with mad hair, made by squeezing colour paste through a garlic press. Easy peasy!

Preheat the oven to 180°C/350°F/gas 4 and put 12 paper cases into a muffin tray. Sieve the flour into a bowl.

Cream the butter, sugar and vanilla in a bowl, using a hand-held electric whisk (or in a free-standing mixer using the whisk attachment), until pale. Scrape down the bowl while whisking. Once the mixture is pale, slowly add the beaten eggs a little at a time while continuing to whisk. Once the eggs have been incorporated, fold in the flour and milk with a large metal spoon – use the 'figure of eight' action – keeping air in the mix until you have an even colour (do not over-mix). The mixture should be of dropping consistency. Spoon the mixture into the paper cases, filling them halfway up, and bake for 15–20 minutes, checking the cupcakes at 12 minutes. They should have risen and the top should feel springy. A wooden skewer stabbed into the sponge should come out clean.

While the cupcakes are cooking, you can start to make the topping. To make the water icing, sift the icing sugar into a bowl and add the water, a little at a time, stirring until you have quite a thick paste but one that is loose enough to pipe or spoon on to the cupcakes. Take out about 100g of the icing and put it into a bowl, then add the red food colour paste a little at a time, on the end of a spoon. Take out another 50g of the icing and colour it black the same way. Colour the white roll-out icing with the green food colour paste by kneading the paste into the icing until you have your desired depth of colour.

When the cupcakes are ready, take them out of the oven and leave them to cool in the tray.

To assemble the clowns, first spread white water icing all over the top of each cupcake. Before it dries, place 2 yellow Smarties on each cake to make the eyes. Set aside for the icing to dry completely, then pipe a big wide smile with the red water icing. Dot pupils on the eyes with black water icing, and pipe in black eyebrows, if you like.

Finally, push the green roll-out icing through a garlic press to make hair and stick it above the eyes.

SPONGE

175g self-raising flour

125g butter

175g caster sugar

1 teaspoon good-quality vanilla extract or essence

2 free-range eggs (50g), beaten

40ml milk

TOPPING

240g white roll-out icing

3–5mm green food colour paste

24 yellow Smarties

For the red and black water icing

420g icing sugar, sifted

6 tablespoons water

3–5mm each of red and black food colour paste

MONSTER CUPCAKE

+ Makes 9 monsters + Prep 15 minutes + Cook 20 minutes + Decorate 45 minutes

I used a vanilla sponge to create these yellow monsters, with textured faces made with yellow vermicelli. Fill the cupcake cases to just below the top before you bake them, so you get a domed shape that helps show the texture of the vermicelli and the monster's bulging face.

SPONGE

175g self-raising flour

125g butter

175g caster sugar

1 teaspoon good-quality vanilla extract or essence

2 free-range eggs (50g), beaten

40ml milk

TOPPING

yellow vermicelli

50g white roll-out icing

For the yellow cream cheese topping

40g very soft butter

80g icing sugar, sifted

120g Philadelphia cream cheese

1 teaspoon good-quality vanilla extract or essence

4–5mm yellow food colour paste

For the black water icing

70g icing sugar, sifted

1 tablespoon water

4–5mm black food colour paste

Preheat the oven to 180°C/350°F/gas 4 and put 12 paper cases into a muffin tray. Sieve the flour into a bowl.

Cream the butter, sugar and vanilla in a bowl, using a hand-held electric whisk (or in a free-standing mixer using the whisk attachment), until pale. Scrape down the bowl while whisking. Once the mixture is pale, slowly add the beaten eggs a little at a time while continuing to whisk. Once the eggs have been incorporated, fold in the flour and milk with a large metal spoon – use the 'figure of eight' action – keeping air in the mix until you have an even colour (do not over-mix). The mixture should be of dropping consistency. Spoon the mixture into the paper cases, filling them to just below the top, and bake in the preheated oven for 15–20 minutes, checking at 12 minutes. The cupcakes should have risen and the top should feel springy. A wooden skewer stabbed into the sponge should come out clean.

For the cream cheese topping, cream the butter and icing sugar together and add the cream cheese and vanilla. Mix until the filling is smooth, but take care not to over-beat or it will become runny. Add the yellow colour paste, a little at a time, on the end of a spoon, and mix until you have a really bright colour to match the vermicelli.

For the black water icing, sift the icing sugar into a bowl and add the water, a little at a time, stirring until you have quite a thick paste but one that is loose enough to pipe or spoon on to the whoopies. Add the black colour paste, a little at a time, on the end of a spoon.

When the cupcakes are ready, take them out of the oven and leave them to cool in the tray.

To assemble each monster, spread the yellow cream cheese topping over the domed cupcake, reserving a little, and sprinkle with the yellow vermicelli. Make 2 bulbous eyes from the white roll-out icing and stick them on to the monster's face with some yellow cream cheese topping. With your black water icing, pipe pupils for the eyes, and draw a wide open mouth.

CELEBRATION WHOOPIES AND CUPCAKES

Cakes have been used in celebrations as far back as Roman times. In fact, traditionally the groom would eat part of the cake and break the rest over his bride's head! It was supposed to bring good luck, but I'm not sure that it would endear modern-day couples to their spouses. Across the world throughout history people have made cakes for celebrations, usually related to religious ceremonies. Here, I have created a few fun celebratory cakes that won't give you a headache!

WHOOPIES

CUPCAKES

VALENTINE'S WHOOPIE

+ Makes 8 whoopies (7–9cm across) + Prep 20 minutes + Cook 8 minutes + Decorate 30 minutes

SPONGE

140g plain flour

40g cocoa powder

1 level teaspoon
    bicarbonate of soda

90ml buttermilk

1 teaspoon good-quality
    vanilla extract or essence

80g butter

140g soft light brown sugar

1 free-range egg (50g),
    beaten

FILLING

50g very soft butter

100g icing sugar, sifted

150g Philadelphia cream
    cheese

1 teaspoon good-quality
    vanilla extract or essence

TOPPING

320g white roll-out icing

2–3mm red food colour
    paste

One of our first bulk orders at the bakery was for 600 Valentine whoopies. We decorated them with bright coloured pink, cerise and red toppings and contrasting pink, red and cerise sprinkles. But my favourite idea is a whoopie made with a heart-shaped cutter. That on a tray with a little glass of pink champagne, delivered on Valentine's morning, is sure to win over the hardest heart!

This recipe uses basic chocolate sponges, but you can also use red velvet recipe on page 26 for a red sponge.

Preheat the oven to 200°C/400°F/gas 6 and line a baking tray with grease-proof paper. Sieve the flour, cocoa powder and bicarbonate of soda into a bowl. Mix the buttermilk with the vanilla and set aside.

Cream the butter and sugar together in a bowl, using a hand-held electric whisk (or in a free-standing mixer using the whisk attachment), until pale. Scrape down the bowl while whisking. Once the mixture is pale, slowly add the beaten egg a little at a time while continuing to whisk. Once the egg has been incorporated, fold in the wet and dry ingredients with a large metal spoon – use the 'figure of eight' action – keeping air in the mix until you have an even colour (do not over-mix). Pipe or spoon 16 x 4cm dollops (at least 4cm high) on to the baking tray, spacing them well apart to allow for spreading, and bake in the preheated oven for 8 minutes.

While the sponges are cooking, you can start to make the filling. Cream the butter and icing sugar together and add the cream cheese and vanilla. Mix until the filling is smooth, but take care not to over-beat or it will become runny.

Take the sponges out of the oven and leave to cool on the tray. When cool, lift them off with a fish slice.

To make heart-shaped whoopies, cut heart shapes out of the whoopie sponge with your heart-shaped cutter and sandwich the hearts together with the vanilla cream cheese filling. Colour the roll-out icing with the red food colour paste by kneading the colour into the paste. Roll out the icing and cut out 8 heart-shaped pieces. Place an icing heart on each heart-shaped whoopie.

And there you have it. They will be fighting over you.

MOTHER'S DAY WHOOPIE

+ Makes 8 whoopies (4–5cm across) + Prep 25 minutes + Cook 6 minutes

I would love to have these little delights given to me as a present on Mother's Day morning, but I haven't got any hope of that happening unless I make them myself! They are so delicious I'm planning to make them as a pudding for a dinner party. Buy the raspberry purée ready-made, or make your own by puréeing ripe raspberries in a blender.

Preheat the oven to 200°C/400°F/gas 6 and line a baking tray with grease-proof paper. Sieve the flour and bicarbonate of soda into a bowl. Stir the colour paste into the raspberry purée and set aside.

Cream the butter and sugar together in a bowl, using a hand-hold electric whisk (or in a free-standing mixer using the whisk attachment), until pale. Scrape down the bowl while whisking. Once the mixture is pale, slowly add the beaten egg a little at a time while continuing to whisk. Once the egg has been incorporated, fold in the wet and dry ingredients with a large metal spoon – use the 'figure of eight' action – keeping air in the mix until you have an even colour (do not over-mix). Pipe or spoon 16 x 3cm dollops (at least 3cm high) on to the baking tray, spacing them well apart to allow for spreading, and bake in the preheated oven for 6 minutes.

While the sponges are cooking, you can start to make the filling. Cream the butter and icing sugar together and add the cream cheese, raspberry purée and crushed raspberries. Mix until the filling is smooth, but take care not to over-beat or it will become runny.

Take the sponges out of the oven and leave to cool on the tray. When cool, lift them off with a fish slice.

To assemble the whoopies, place 8 sponges curved side down and spoon or pipe some of the raspberry cream cheese filling in the centre. Stand 5 fresh raspberries around the edge of the filling, using it to help hold the raspberries in place. Top each one with another sponge. Pipe or spoon a dollop of the raspberry cream cheese filling on top of each whoopie and finish with a raspberry.

SPONGE
100g plain flour

1 level teaspoon bicarbonate of soda

1 teaspoon red food colour paste

20ml raspberry purée

40g butter

75g caster sugar

1 free-range egg (50g), beaten

FILLING AND TOPPING
10g very soft butter

45g icing sugar, sifted

60g Philadelphia cream cheese

10ml raspberry purée

6 crushed raspberries

48 fresh raspberries

EASTER BONNET WHOOPIE

Easter is such a happy time of the year. Winter is over, we have a four-day bank holiday from work, the children are off school, and what better way to occupy them than by getting them to help you make these lovely Easter delights.

SPONGE

100g plain flour

1 level teaspoon
   bicarbonate of soda

20ml buttermilk

1 teaspoon good-quality
   vanilla extract or essence

40g butter

50g caster sugar

1 free-range egg (50g),
   beaten

FILLING

60g very soft butter

120g icing sugar, sifted

1 teaspoon good-quality
   vanilla extract or essence

raspberry jam

TOPPING

200g white roll-out icing

2–3mm yellow food
   colour paste

thin white ribbons

For the yellow water icing

50g icing sugar, sifted

1 tablespoon water

a little yellow food
   colour paste

Preheat the oven to 200°C/400°F/gas 6 and line 2 baking trays with grease-proof paper. Sieve the flour and bicarbonate of soda into a bowl. Mix the buttermilk with the vanilla and set aside.

Cream the butter and sugar together in a bowl, using a hand-held electric whisk (or in a free-standing mixer using the whisk attachment), until pale. Scrape down the bowl while whisking. Once the mixture is pale, slowly add the beaten egg a little at a time while continuing to whisk. Once the egg has been incorporated, fold in the wet and dry ingredients with a large metal spoon – use the 'figure of eight' action – keeping air in the mix until you have an even colour (do not over-mix). Pipe or spoon 8 x 3cm dollops (at least 3cm high) on to a baking tray, spacing them well apart to allow for spreading, and bake in the preheated oven for 8 minutes. On another tray pipe or spoon 8 x 2cm dollops (at least 2cm high) and bake for 5–7 minutes.

Take the sponges out of the oven and leave to cool on the trays. When cool, lift them off with a fish slice. For the filling, cream the butter, icing sugar and vanilla together and beat until smooth, but do not over-beat or it will become runny. To make the water icing, sift the icing sugar into a bowl and add the water, a little at a time, stirring until you have quite a thick paste but one that is loose enough to pipe or spoon on to the whoopies. Add the yellow food colour paste on the end of a spoon. Cut off 50g of the roll-out icing and set aside. Colour the remaining icing with the yellow colour paste by kneading the paste into the icing.

To assemble, place one of the larger sponge halves flat side down and spread with raspberry jam and some of the butter icing filling. Stick one of the smaller halves on top, then coat both sponges in a thin layer of butter icing.

Divide the yellow roll-out icing into 8 equal balls. Dust the work surface with icing sugar and roll out one of the balls of icing to a 10cm diameter circle. Lifting the circle of icing carefully, cover the bonnet tightly with it. Roll out the reserved white roll-out icing and make little flowers with a flower-shaped pastry cutter. Place them on the bonnet and fix in place with yellow water icing. Use yellow water icing to dot a little centre in the middle of each flower.

CHRISTENING WHOOPIE

+ Makes 12 whoopies (4–5cm across)   + Prep 20 minutes   + Cook 6 minutes   + Decorate 1½ hours

Whether your christening is in summer or winter, these are a great accompaniment. They would also work brilliantly as a new baby present: although the baby won't be able to eat them, the mum will really appreciate them!

Preheat the oven to 200°C/400°F/gas 6 and line a baking tray with grease-proof paper. Sieve the flour and bicarbonate of soda into a bowl. Mix the buttermilk with the vanilla and set aside.

Cream the butter and sugar together in a bowl, using a hand-held electric whisk (or in a free-standing mixer using the whisk attachment), until pale. Scrape down the bowl while whisking. Once the mixture is pale, slowly add the beaten egg a little at a time while continuing to whisk. Once the egg has been incorporated, fold in the wet and dry ingredients with a large metal spoon – use the 'figure of eight' action – keeping air in the mix until you have an even colour (do not over-mix). Pipe or spoon 24 x 3cm dollops (at least 3cm high) on to the baking tray, spacing them well apart to allow for spreading, and bake in the preheated oven for 6 minutes.

While the sponges are cooking, you can make the filling. Cream the butter, icing sugar and vanilla together and beat until smooth. Cut off half the roll-out icing and set aside. Colour the remaining icing with the colour paste by kneading the paste into the icing until you have your desired depth of colour. For the water icing, sift the icing sugar into a bowl and add the water, a little at a time, stirring until you have quite a thick paste.

Take the sponges out of the oven and leave to cool on the tray. When cool, lift them off with a fish slice.

To assemble the christening cakes, sandwich the sponges together with some of the the butter icing filling and a thin layer of raspberry jam. Cover the whoopies lightly with more butter icing.

Divide the coloured roll-out icing into approximately 35g balls. Dust a work surface with icing sugar and roll out one of the balls to a 10cm diameter circle. Lifting the circle of icing carefully, drape it over one of your whoopies and fix it in place. Roll out the reserved white icing and cut out the letters 'ABC' or the numbers '123'. Fix them on top with a little white water icing. Make the rest of the christening cakes in the same way.

SPONGE

200g plain flour

1 level teaspoon bicarbonate of soda

50ml buttermilk

1 teaspoon good-quality vanilla extract or essence

80g butter

100g caster sugar

1 free-range egg (50g), beaten

FILLING

90g very soft butter

150g icing sugar, sifted

1 teaspoon good-quality vanilla extract or essence

50g raspberry jam

TOPPING

480g white roll-out icing

2–3mm baby pink or baby blue food colour paste

For the white water icing

50g icing sugar, sifted

1 tablespoon water

WEDDING WHOOPIE

+ Makes 8 whoopies (7–9cm across) + Prep time 25 minutes + Cook time 30 minutes

This sponge recipe is the one used for my bakery's award-winning lemon drizzle cupcake, the Crazy Lemon Drizzle (see page 112). I've adapted it for whoopie production, and because it's so special I think it works brilliantly as a wedding cake. The sharp citrus sponge with its very lemony white set topping tastes sublime. A small piece of silver leaf (which you can buy from www.goldleafsupplies.co.uk) on each whoopie adds a modern twist.

SPONGE

180g plain flour

1 level teaspoon
 bicarbonate of soda

45g buttermilk

90g soft butter

140g caster sugar

zest of 2 lemons

1 free-range egg (50g),
 beaten

For the lemon drizzle

juice of 2 lemons

50g icing sugar

FILLING

65g very soft butter

130g icing sugar, sifted

200g Philadelphia
 cream cheese

10ml lemon juice

TOPPING

210g icing sugar

6 tablespoons lemon juice

a sheet of silver leaf, or a
 few gold or silver balls

Preheat the oven to 200°C/400°F/gas 6 and line a baking tray with grease-proof paper. Sieve the flour and bicarbonate of soda into a bowl. Put the buttermilk into a jug and set aside.

Cream the butter, sugar and lemon zest together in a bowl, using a hand-held electric whisk (or in a free-standing mixer using the whisk attachment), until pale. Scrape down the bowl while whisking. Once the mixture is pale, slowly add the beaten egg a little at a time while continuing to whisk. Once the egg has been incorporated, fold in the wet and dry ingredients with a large metal spoon – use the 'figure of eight' action – keeping air in the mix until you have an even colour (do not over-mix). Pipe or spoon 16 x 4cm dollops (at least 4cm high) on to the baking tray, spacing them well apart to allow for spreading, and bake in the preheated oven for 8 minutes, taking care they do not start to get too much colour on top.

While the sponges are cooking, make the lemon drizzle by mixing the lemon juice with the icing sugar. Now you can start to make the filling. Cream the butter and icing sugar together and add the cream cheese and lemon juice. Mix until the filling is smooth, but take care not to over-beat or it will become runny. For the topping, sift the icing sugar into a bowl and add the lemon juice, a little at a time, stirring until you have quite a thick paste but one that is loose enough to pipe or spoon on to the whoopies.

Take the sponges out of the oven and leave to cool on the tray. When cool, lift them off with a fish slice. Drizzle them with the lemon drizzle mix and set aside for about 2 hours to dry. Sandwich them together with the lemon cream cheese filling and top with the lemon water icing. Finish with a piece of silver leaf or a gold or silver ball.

BIRTHDAY WHOOPIE

+ Makes 13 whoopies (4–5cm across) + Prep 20 minutes + Cook 8 minutes + Decorate 30 minutes

In the seventeenth century, European cakes started to look a bit more like our birthday cakes today, i.e. round, with a topping and a filling. But only the really wealthy could afford cakes with elaborate layers. Whoopies make fantastic birthday cakes. You can choose your preferred sponge from one of the other chapters, or make one of the characters in the Wacky Whoopie chapter, or simply decorate each whoopie with bright-coloured water icing and write 'HAPPY BIRTHDAY', with one letter on each cake.

Preheat the oven to 200°C/400°F/gas 6 and line a baking tray with grease-proof paper. Sieve the flour, cocoa powder and bicarbonate of soda into a bowl. Mix the buttermilk with the vanilla and set aside.

Cream the butter and sugar together in a bowl, using a hand-held electric whisk (or in a free-standing mixer using the whisk attachment), until pale. Scrape down the bowl while whisking. Once the mixture is pale, slowly add the beaten egg a little at a time while continuing to whisk. Once the egg has been incorporated, fold in the wet and dry ingredients with a large metal spoon – use the 'figure of eight' action – keeping air in the mix until you have an even colour (do not over mix). Pipe or spoon 16 x 3cm dollops (at least 3cm high) on to the baking tray, spacing them well apart to allow for spreading, and bake in the preheated oven for 8 minutes.

While the sponges are cooking, you can start to make the filling. Cream the butter and icing sugar together, then add the cream cheese and vanilla. Mix until the filling is smooth, but take care not to over-beat or it will become runny. For the topping, sift the icing sugar into a bowl and add the water, a little at a time, stirring until you have quite a thick paste but one that is loose enough to pipe or spoon on to the whoopies. Divide the water icing between 6 different bowls and colour 5 of them each with a different colour paste, adding it a little at a time, on the end of a spoon. Leave one batch of icing white, to use for the writing.

Take the sponges out of the oven and leave to cool on the tray. When cool, lift them off with a fish slice. Sandwich them together with the classic cream cheese filling and spread or pipe the coloured water icing on top. Place the whoopies on a tray or a cake-board and write a letter on each cake, to spell out 'HAPPY BIRTHDAY'.

SPONGE

140g plain flour

40g cocoa powder

1 level teaspoon bicarbonate of soda

90ml buttermilk

1 teaspoon good-quality vanilla extract or essence

80g butter

140g soft light brown sugar

1 free-range egg (50g), beaten

FILLING

50g very soft butter

100g icing sugar, sifted

150g Philadelphia cream cheese

1 teaspoon good-quality vanilla extract or essence

TOPPING

280g icing sugar, sifted

4 tablespoons water

2–3mm of food colour paste in each of 5 different colours

FATHER'S DAY WHOOPIE

+ Makes 8 whoopies (7–9cm across) + Prep 1½ hours + Cook 8 minutes + Decorate 30 minutes

Tell your dad he is a star on Father's Day by making him these whoopies. Also great for celebrating the Fourth of July if you're American. We have some friends who throw a Fourth of July party every year, and this one is for them. The whoopies are wrapped in white, red and blue roll-out icing, with florist's wire stars.

SPONGE
140g plain flour

40g cocoa powder

1 level teaspoon
   bicarbonate of soda

90ml buttermilk

1 teaspoon good-quality
   vanilla extract or essence

80g butter

140g soft light brown sugar

1 free-range egg (50g),
   beaten

FILLING
50g very soft butter

100g icing sugar, sifted

150g Philadelphia
   cream cheese

1 teaspoon good-quality
   vanilla extract or essence

TOPPING
480g white roll-out icing

2–3mm each of red and
   blue food colour paste

florist's wire

Start by making the stars. Divide the roll-out icing into 3 balls. Add the red colour paste to the first ball and the blue to the second, kneading the paste into the icing until you have your desired depth of colour. Leave the third ball white. Dust a work surface with icing sugar and roll out a 40g piece of icing in each colour. Cut out stars and set them aside to dry for about an hour. You'll need 3–6 stars per whoopie.

Preheat the oven to 200°C/400°F/gas 6 and line a baking tray with grease-proof paper. Sieve the flour, cocoa powder and bicarbonate of soda into a bowl. Mix the buttermilk with the vanilla and set aside.

Cream the butter and sugar together in a bowl, using a hand-held electric whisk (or in a free-standing mixer using the whisk attachment), until pale. Scrape down the bowl while whisking. Once the mixture is pale, slowly add the beaten egg a little at a time while continuing to whisk. Once the egg has been incorporated, fold in the wet and dry ingredients with a large metal spoon – use the 'figure of eight' action – keeping air in the mix until you have an even colour (do not over-mix). Pipe or spoon 16 x 4cm dollops (at least 4cm high) on to the baking tray, spacing them well apart to allow for spreading, and bake in the preheated oven for 8 minutes.

Cream the butter and icing sugar together and add the cream cheese and vanilla. Mix until the filling is smooth, but take care not to over-beat or it will become runny. Take the sponges out of the oven and leave to cool on the tray. When cool, lift them off with a fish slice.

To assemble the whoopies, sandwich the sponges together with some of the cream cheese filling. Then coat the whoopies with more of the filling. Dust a work surface with icing sugar. Divide the remaining red, white and blue icing into 45g balls and roll one of them out to a 15cm diameter circle. Lifting the circle of icing carefully, drape it over a whoopie and fix it in place. Attach the stars to pieces of florist's wire and stick them in the top. Make the rest of the whoopies in the same way.

HALLOWE'EN WHOOPIES

Hallowe'en is linked to the Celts, who celebrated the end of the summer, the light half of the year, and the beginning of the darker half. They believed that on this day we come closer to the 'Otherworld'. Here are some suitable whoopies to help you celebrate this spooky day. These evil faces and ghosts are so simple to make, and so effective. When making the evil whoopies a good tip is to have a paintbrush to hand.

EVIL FACE WHOOPIE
+ Makes 8 evil faces + Prep 20 minutes + Cook 8 minutes + Decorate 1 hour

SPONGE

140g plain flour

40g cocoa powder

1 level teaspoon bicarbonate of soda

90ml buttermilk

1 teaspoon good-quality vanilla extract or essence

80g butter

140g soft light brown sugar

1 free-range egg (50g), beaten

FILLING

50g very soft butter

100g icing sugar, sifted

150g Philadelphia cream cheese

1 teaspoon good-quality vanilla extract or essence

2–3mm red food colour paste

Preheat the oven to 200°C/400°F/gas 6 and line a baking tray with grease-proof paper. Sieve the flour, cocoa powder and bicarbonate of soda into a bowl. Mix the buttermilk with the vanilla and set aside.

Cream the butter and sugar together in a bowl, using a hand-held electric whisk (or in a free-standing mixer using the whisk attachment), until pale. Scrape down the bowl while whisking. Once the mixture is pale, slowly add the beaten egg a little at a time while continuing to whisk. Once the egg has been incorporated, fold in the wet and dry ingredients with a large metal spoon – use the 'figure of eight' action – keeping air in the mix until you have an even colour (do not over-mix). Pipe or spoon 16 x 4cm dollops (at least 4cm high) on to the baking tray, spacing them well apart to allow for spreading, and bake for 8 minutes.

While the sponges are cooking you can start to make the filling. Cream the butter and icing sugar together and add the cream cheese and vanilla. Mix until the filling is smooth, but take care not to over-beat or it will become runny. Take out 50g of the filling and set aside. Then add the colour paste to the rest, a little at a time, on the end of a spoon, and mix until you have a lovely bright strong red.

For the water icing, sift the icing sugar into a bowl and add the water, a little at a time, stirring until you have quite a thick paste but one that is loose enough to pipe or spoon on to the whoopies. Take out a little of the topping and set aside. Then add the red colour paste to the rest, a little at a time, on the end of a spoon.

Take the sponges out of the oven and leave to cool on the tray. When cool, lift them off with a fish slice.

To assemble the evil faces, sandwich the sponges together with the red cream cheese filling. Spread a little of the white cream cheese filling over the top of each whoopie. Set aside 100g of the white roll-out icing for the eyes and mouth and divide the remainder into 8 balls about 45g each. Dust a work surface with icing sugar and roll out one of the balls into a 10cm diameter circle. Lifting the circle of icing carefully, place it on top of one of the whoopies. Make the rest of the whoopies in the same way.

Now you are ready to make your white whoopies into evil faces. Paint the underneath of each whoopie with black food paste so you can't see any white. Be careful – place them on a piece of greaseproof paper so you don't get black food colour everywhere. Then finish painting the top, so they are completely black, and leave them to dry for 30 minutes.

In the meantime, make the mouth and eyes from the reserved 100g of roll-out icing. Break off 8 pieces of icing and roll them out into 5mm wide round balls, flattening them slightly. Dust your work surface with icing sugar, roll out the rest of the white icing and cut out 4 strips measuring 4 x 1cm. Cut a zigzag shape on one side of the strip to make teeth. Place 2 eyes and a mouth on each evil face. Make a red pupil with a dot of red water icing, and zigzag more red water icing around the teeth.

TOPPING

460g white roll-out icing

1–2 teaspoons black food colour paste

For the red and white water icing

140g icing sugar, sifted

2 tablespoons water

2–3mm red food colour paste

GHOST WHOOPIE
+ Makes 4 ghosts | Prep 10 minutes + Cook 8 minutes + Decorate 20 minutes

I used a basic chocolate sponge and filling, as used for the evil faces (see opposite), but you can use your favourite sponge.

To assemble the ghosts, sandwich the larger sponges together with the filling. Place the whoopies on your work surface. Using your filling as glue, fix one of the smaller sponges flat side down on top of each whoopie, with another one on top to make a tower.

Cut off a 20g piece of the white roll-out icing and colour it with the black colour paste by kneading the colour into the paste. Divide the rest of the white roll-out icing into 4 equal 50g balls. Dust a work surface with icing sugar and roll out one of the balls to a 14cm diameter circle. Lifting the circle of icing carefully, drape it over one of your whoopie towers. Your ghost has risen. All he needs is two black eyes. Roll out the black roll-out icing on your work surface and cut out the eyes with the top of a tomato purée tube. Glue them in place with a little icing sugar mixed with water. Make 3 more ghosts in the same way.

SPONGE

8 x 7–9cm whoopie bases

4 x 4–5cm whoopie bases

TOPPING

220g white roll-out icing

2–3mm black food colour paste

GUY FAWKES WHOOPIE

+ Makes 6–7 whoopies (7–9cm across) + Prep 15 minutes + Cook 8 minutes + Decorate 10 minutes

These whoopies taste great and are really eye-catching, with a beautiful bright orange 'bonfire' on top – perfect for any Guy Fawkes night party. You can buy the pumpkin purée, but I've also given instructions for making it yourself.

SPONGE

125g plain flour

½ level teaspoon
bicarbonate of soda

1 level teaspoon
ground cinnamon

1 level teaspoon
ground ginger

a pinch of ground cloves

100g soft light brown sugar

60ml sunflower oil

100g pumpkin purée
(see method)

FILLING

65g very soft butter

130g icing sugar, sifted

200g Philadelphia
cream cheese

2 teaspoons good-quality
vanilla extract or essence

2–3mm orange food colour
paste (more if you want
a really strong colour)

TOPPING

4 x 39g packets of Mikado
biscuits or Matchmakers

First make the pumpkin purée. Preheat the oven to 180°C/350°F/gas 4. Cut a pumpkin into pieces, leaving the skin on and scraping away the seeds and stringy bits. Put the pumpkin pieces on a baking tray and roast them in the preheated oven for 2 hours. Leave to cool a bit, then scoop out the flesh and purée it in a food processor. You need 100g for this recipe – use the rest to make a soup for your bonfire party.

Preheat the oven to 190°C/375°F/gas 5. Sieve the flour, bicarbonate of soda, cinnamon, ginger and cloves into a bowl and stir in the sugar. Mix the oil with the pumpkin purée. Mix the wet ingredients with the dry ingredients and fold in with a large metal spoon – use the 'figure of eight' action – keeping air in the mix until you have an even colour (do not over-mix). Pipe or spoon 12–14 x 4cm dollops (at least 4cm high) on to the baking tray, spacing them well apart to allow for spreading, and bake in the preheated oven for 8 minutes.

While the sponges are cooking, you can start to make the filling. Cream the butter and icing sugar together and add the cream cheese and vanilla. Mix until the filling is smooth, but take care not to over-beat or it will become runny. Add the colour paste, a little at a time, on the end of a spoon.

Take the sponges out of the oven and leave to cool on the tray. When cool, lift them off with a fish slice. Sandwich them together with the orange cream cheese filling and pipe a swirl of the filling on top, making peaks so it looks like a fire. Chop the Mikado biscuits or Matchmakers so you get a mixture of short and long twigs, and arrange them on top like a bonfire.

SNOWMAN WHOOPIE

+Makes 6 snowmen   +Prep 25 minutes   +Cook 8 minutes   +Decorate 1 hour

I have chosen a gingerbread sponge for this spicy snowman whoopie, filled
with a vanilla cream cheese filling. Best eaten by the fire while watching a
Christmas film – probably *The Wizard of Oz* again!

Preheat the oven to 200°C/400°F/gas 6 and line a baking tray with grease-proof paper. Sieve the flour, ginger, cinnamon and bicarbonate of soda into a bowl. Mix the buttermilk with the treacle and golden syrup and set aside.

Cream the butter, sugar and orange zest together in a bowl, using a hand-held electric whisk (or in a free-standing mixer using the whisk attachment), until pale. Scrape down the bowl while whisking. Once the mixture is pale, slowly add the beaten egg a little at a time while continuing to whisk. Once the egg has been incorporated, fold in the wet and dry ingredients with a large metal spoon – use the 'figure of eight' action – keeping air in the mix until you have an even colour (do not over-mix). Pipe or spoon 18 x 3cm dollops (at least 3cm high) and 6 x ½cm dollops for the hat on to the baking tray, spacing them well apart to allow for spreading, and bake in the preheated oven for 8 minutes.

Cream the butter and icing sugar together and add the cream cheese. Mix until the filling is smooth but take care not to over-beat or it will become runny.

Cut off about 20g of the white roll-out icing and colour it orange by kneading the colour paste into the icing until you have your desired depth of colour. Cut off another 50g of icing and colour it red in the same way. For the black water icing, sift the icing sugar into a bowl and add the water a little at a time until you have quite a thick paste that is loose enough to pipe or spoon on to the snowman. Add the food colour paste on the end of a spoon.

Take the sponges out of the oven and leave to cool on the tray. When cool, lift them off with a fish slice.

To assemble each snowman, take 3 sponges, slice the top off one and sandwich it between the other 2 sponges with some of the cream cheese filling to make the body of the snowman. Coat the body lightly with more of the filling.

Cut off a 25g ball of white roll-out icing, then dust a work surface with icing sugar and roll it out to a 12cm diameter circle. Lifting the circle of icing carefully, drape it over the body of the snowman. Take a 20g ball of icing and roll it into a ball to make the head. Take a little of the orange roll-out icing and make a nose.

Roll out a strip of red roll-out icing for the belt. Make grooves in the belt by rolling the top of a tomato purée tube along it. Stick on the head and belt and add 2 M&Ms for the buttons. With the black water icing, pipe on 2 eyes and a mouth, and finish with a small whoopie.

There you have your smiley fellow.

SPONGE

125g plain flour

1 level teaspoon ground ginger

1 level teaspoon ground cinnamon

1 level tablespoon bicarbonate of soda

25ml buttermilk

25g treacle

20g golden syrup

50g butter

45g soft dark brown sugar

zest of ½ an orange

1 free-range egg (50g), beaten

FILLING

25g very soft butter

50g icing sugar, sifted

75g Philadelphia cream cheese

TOPPING

330g white roll-out icing

2–3mm each of red and orange food colour paste

12 M&Ms

For the black water icing

70g icing sugar, sifted

1 tablespoon water

2–3mm black food colour paste

VALENTINE'S CUPCAKE

+ Makes 12 cupcakes + Prep 15 minutes + Cook 20 minutes + Decorate 25 minutes

For this cupcake I've chosen a red velvet sponge decorated with red water icing and a heart cut out of white or pink roll-out icing. It is so simple but really effective. It would also work well using a chocolate sponge and chocolate cream cheese icing. Whatever your loved one prefers!

SPONGE

145g self-raising flour

30g cocoa powder

125g butter

175g caster sugar

1 teaspoon good-quality vanilla extract or essence

2 free-range eggs (50g), beaten

2 tablespoons milk

4 teaspoons liquid red food colouring (Dr Oetker)

TOPPING

60g white roll-out icing

For the red water icing

280g icing sugar

4 tablespoons water

2–3mm red food colour paste

Preheat the oven to 180°C/350°F/gas 4 and put 12 paper cases into a muffin tray. Sieve the flour and cocoa into a bowl.

Cream the butter, sugar and vanilla in a bowl, using a hand-held electric whisk (or in a free-standing mixer using the whisk attachment), until pale. Scrape down the bowl while whisking. Once the mixture is pale, slowly add the beaten eggs a little at a time while continuing to whisk. Once the eggs have been incorporated, fold in the flour, milk and food colouring with a large metal spoon – use the 'figure of eight' action – keeping air in the mix until you have an even colour (do not over-mix). The mixture should be of dropping consistency. Spoon the mixture into the paper cases, filling them halfway up, and bake in the preheated oven for 15–20 minutes, checking at 12 minutes. They should have risen and the top should feel springy. A wooden skewer stabbed into the sponge should come out clean.

While the cupcakes are cooking you can start to make the water icing. Sift the icing sugar into a bowl and add the water, a little at a time, stirring until you have quite a thick paste but one that is loose enough to pipe or spoon on to the whoopies. Add the red colour paste, a little at a time, on the end of a spoon.

Dust a work surface with icing sugar, then roll out the white roll-out icing and cut out 12 hearts.

When the cupcakes are ready, take them out of the oven and leave them to cool in the tray. Top each cupcake with the red water icing and place a heart immediately on top before the icing dries.

EASTER NEST CUPCAKE

+ Makes 12 cupcakes + Prep 15 minutes + Cook 20 minutes + Decorate 20 minutes

This is a perfect spring cupcake, using a simple vanilla sponge and a basket of brown icing piped on to the cake to look like a nest. A great Easter Day treat.

Preheat the oven to 180°C/350°F/gas 4 and put 12 paper cases into a muffin tray. Sieve the flour into a bowl.

Cream the butter, sugar and vanilla in a bowl, using a hand-held electric whisk (or in a free standing mixer using the whisk attachment), until pale. Scrape down the bowl while whisking. Once the mixture is pale, slowly add the beaten eggs a little at a time while continuing to whisk. Once the eggs have been incorporated, fold in the flour and milk with a large metal spoon – use the 'figure of eight' action – keeping air in the mix until you have an even colour (do not over mix). The mixture should be of dropping consistency. Spoon the mixture into the paper cases, filling them halfway up, and bake in the preheated oven for 15–20 minutes, checking at 12 minutes. They should have risen and the top should feel springy. A wooden skewer stabbed into the sponge should come out clean.

While the cupcakes are cooking you can start to make the topping. Cream the butter, icing sugar and cocoa powder together and mix until the icing is smooth.

When the cupcakes are ready, take them out of the oven and leave them to cool in the tray. Spread them with the chocolate butter icing, then pipe a little circle of icing on top of each one to look like a bird's nest. Place 3 mini eggs in each nest.

SPONGE

175g self-raising flour

125g butter

175g caster sugar

2 free-range eggs (50g), beaten

1 teaspoon good-quality vanilla extract or essence

40ml milk

TOPPING

150g very soft butter

250g icing sugar, sifted

30g cocoa powder

1 packet of mini Easter eggs

WEDDING CUPCAKE

+ Makes 12 cupcakes + Prep 30 minutes + Cook 20 minutes + Decorate 1 hour

I have decorated this cupcake with a single rosebud, but you can use two or three, or add leaves as you wish. The rosebuds really are easy to make, and I've included instructions, but you can buy them if you are too nervous to try. If you want a pure white cake, use a white chocolate sponge (see page 89), and make a white rose to match.

SPONGE
175g self-raising flour
1 teaspoon red food colour paste
40ml raspberry purée
125g butter
125g caster sugar
1 teaspoon good-quality vanilla extract or essence
2 free-range eggs (50g), beaten
50ml milk

TOPPING
100g white chocolate
50g very soft butter
50g icing sugar, sifted
100g Philadelphia cream cheese
120g pink roll-out icing

Preheat the oven to 180°C/350°F/gas 4 and put 12 paper cases into a muffin tray. Sieve the flour into a bowl. Mix the red colour paste into the raspberry purée and set aside.

Cream the butter, sugar and vanilla in a bowl, using a hand-held electric whisk (or in a free-standing mixer using the whisk attachment), until pale. Scrape down the bowl while whisking. Once the mixture is pale, slowly add the beaten eggs a little at a time while continuing to whisk. Once the eggs have been incorporated, fold in the flour with a large metal spoon – use the 'figure of eight' action – keeping air in the mix until you have an even colour (do not over-mix). Then fold in the raspberry purée. The mixture should be of dropping consistency.

Spoon the mixture into the paper cases, filling them halfway up, and bake in the preheated oven for 15–20 minutes, checking at 12 minutes. The cupcakes should have risen and the top should feel springy. A wooden skewer stabbed into the sponge should come out clean.

Melt the white chocolate in a glass bowl over a saucepan of barely simmering water and set aside to cool. Cream the butter and icing sugar together. Add the cream cheese plus the cooled white chocolate and beat really fast. Mix until the topping is smooth, but take care not to over-beat or it will become runny.

To make a rosebud, take about 10g of pink roll-out icing and roll it into an even sausage. Now divide it into 4 even sausage rolls. Flatten each sausage at one end, leaving the other end fat. The thin end is the top of the petal, the fat end the bottom. Take your first petal and make it into a cone, flat side up, then place the other petals around it to form a bud. Repeat until you have made 12 rosebuds.

When the cupcakes are ready, take them out of the oven and leave them to cool in the tray. Spread the white chocolate topping in a smooth, flat layer over each cupcake and place a rosebud in the centre.

HALLOWE'EN DRACULA CUPCAKE
+ Makes 12 cupcakes + Prep 15 minutes + Cook 20 minutes + Decorate 30 minutes

I remember seeing Christopher Lee in the Dracula films – I used to be so scared I would make my dad stay with me while I watched. I have made this scary Dracula cupcake with a chocolate sponge, but a red velvet one would work really well too. With his pale face and red glacé cherry eyes he could honour any Hallowe'en party.

Preheat the oven to 180°C/350°F/gas 4 and put 12 paper cases into a muffin tray. Sieve the flour and cocoa powder into a bowl.

Cream the butter, sugar and vanilla in a bowl, using a hand-held electric whisk (or in a free-standing mixer using the whisk attachment), until pale. Scrape down the bowl while whisking. Once the mixture is pale, slowly add the beaten eggs a little at a time while continuing to whisk. Once the eggs have been incorporated, fold in the flour and milk with a large metal spoon – use the 'figure of eight' action – keeping air in the mix until you have an even colour (do not over-mix). The mixture should be of dropping consistency. Spoon the mixture into the paper cases, filling them halfway up, and bake in the preheated oven for 15–20 minutes, checking the cupcakes at 12 minutes. They should have risen and the top should feel springy. A wooden skewer stabbed into the sponge should come out clean.

While the cupcakes are cooking, you can start to make the topping. Sift the icing sugar into a bowl and add the water, a little at a time, stirring until you have quite a thick paste but one that is loose enough to pipe or spoon on to the cupcakes. Take out about 120g of the icing and put it into a separate bowl. Add the black food colour paste, a little at a time, on the end of a spoon.

When the cupcakes are ready, take them out of the oven and leave them to cool in the tray.

To finish your Dracula cupcakes, cut the glacé cherries into quarters. Spread the white water icing over each cupcake and then, before it dries, place 2 cherry quarters on each cake for the eyes and place the fangs in position. Set aside for the icing to dry completely, then pipe eyebrows with the black water icing. Draw a black widow's peak above the eyebrows, and dot black pupils on the eyes.

SPONGE
125g self-raising flour
50g cocoa powder
125g butter
175g caster sugar
1 teaspoon good-quality vanilla extract or essence
2 free-range eggs (50g), beaten
40ml milk

TOPPING
6 glacé cherries

For the white and black water icing
420g icing sugar, sifted
6 tablespoons water
3–5mm black food colour paste

CHRISTMAS CUPCAKE

+Makes 6 cupcakes +Prep 24 hours +Cook 40 minutes +Decorate 45 minutes

I love Christmas cake! No one else eats it in our family, though, and sometimes a whole Christmas cake can be a bit much. Making Christmas cupcakes is such a great solution. I can have one and then offer them to guests (with equally good taste!) who drop in over the Christmas period.

SPONGE

15g mixed peel

80g sultanas

80g raisins

80g currants

zest of ½ of an orange

zest of ½ of a lemon

2 tablespoons brandy

100g self-raising flour

½ teaspoon mixed spice

½ teaspoon grated nutmeg

½ teaspoon cinnamon

20g glacé cherries, quartered

75g unsalted butter

50g soft light brown sugar

2 free-range egg (50g), beaten

20g blanched almonds, chopped

1 tablespoon black treacle

TOPPING

90g white roll-out icing

2–3mm each of red and green food colour paste

a little apricot jam

120g almond paste

For the royal icing

250g icing sugar

1 free-range egg white (50g)

2 teaspoons lemon juice

Put the mixed peel, sultanas, raisins, currants and orange, lemon zest and brandy into a bowl. Leave to soak for a few hours, preferably overnight.

Preheat the oven to 140°C/275°F/gas 1 and put 6 paper cases into a muffin tray. Sieve the flour and spices into a bowl. Chop the cherries and add to the flour – a coating of flour will prevent the cherries sinking to the bottom of the cupcake case.

Cream the butter and sugar in a bowl, using a hand-held electric whisk (or in a free-standing mixer using the whisk attachment), until pale. Scrape down the bowl while whisking. Once the mixture is pale, slowly add the beaten egg a little at a time while continuing to whisk. Once the egg has been incorporated, gradually fold in the soaked fruit, nuts, treacle and flour with a large metal spoon – use the 'figure of eight' action – keeping air in the mix until you have an even colour (do not over-mix) and dropping consistency. Spoon the mixture into the paper cases, filling them halfway up, and bake for 35–40 minutes until risen and springy. A wooden skewer stabbed into the sponge should come out clean.

While the cupcakes are cooking, you can start to make the decorations. Divide the white roll-out icing in half and colour one half red and the other green by kneading the paste into the icing until you have your desired depth of colour. Dust a work surface with icing sugar, then roll out the icing and cut tree shapes with a pastry cutter. Set aside to firm up.

When the cupcakes are ready, take them out of the oven and leave them to cool in the tin. Paint the top of each cupcake with apricot jam. Dust the work surface with icing sugar and roll out the almond paste. Cut out circles to fit each cupcake, using a pastry cutter, and place them over the jam.

To make the royal icing for the topping, sift the icing sugar into a bowl and stir in the egg white. Add the lemon juice to taste, but not too much – the icing should be quite stiff. Spoon it on to each cupcake and use the back of a knife to make peaks. Before the icing sets, stand 3 Christmas trees on each cupcake. Happy Christmas!

SPECIALIST WHOOPIES AND CUPCAKES

Out of the six girlfriends I was at college with, three have developed an intolerance to wheat over the years, and many people nowadays are coeliac and can't tolerate gluten. As well as wheat, allergies to nuts and eggs are becoming more and more prevalent. I could almost dedicate a chapter of whoopies to each allergy, but I have chosen a few of my favourite recipes for the most common ones. I have also provided a recipe for a whoopie with no added sugar, so it is suitable for toddlers (and can also be used as a base for recipes in the wacky or celebration chapters for a birthday party or special occasion).

WHOOPIES

CUPCAKES

EGG-FREE APPLE, PLUM AND CINNAMON WHOOPIE

+ Makes 8 whoopies (7–9cm across) + Prep 20 minutes + Cook 8 minutes

When a person suffers from an egg allergy, the body thinks it is being invaded by the proteins in the egg, resulting in breathing problems, hives, stomach aches and head-aches. This is the perfect recipe for people with an egg allergy, and the bonus is that it is also vegetarian.

SPONGE

175g spelt flour

1 level teaspoon
    ground ginger

1 level teaspoon
    ground cinnamon

1 level teaspoon
    bicarbonate of soda

75ml Greek yoghurt

65ml sunflower oil

50g stoned plums,
    finely chopped

50g sharp green eating
    apple, grated

75g caster sugar

FILLING

50g very soft butter

100g icing sugar, sifted

150g Philadelphia
    cream cheese

1 teaspoon good-quality
    vanilla extract or essence

TOPPING

50g icing sugar, sifted

½ level teaspoon cinnamon

Preheat the oven to 200°C/400°F/gas 6 and line a baking tray with grease-proof paper. Sieve the flour, ginger, cinnamon and bicarbonate of soda into a bowl. Mix the yoghurt with the oil.

Add the chopped plums and grated apple to the dry ingredients and fold in the wet ingredients with a large metal spoon – use the 'figure of eight' action – keeping air in the mix until you have an even colour (do not over-mix). Pipe or spoon 16 x 4cm dollops (at least 4cm high) on to the baking tray, spacing them well apart to allow for spreading, and bake in the preheated oven for 8 minutes.

While the sponges are cooking, you can start to make the filling. Cream the butter and icing sugar together and add the cream cheese and vanilla. Mix until the filling is smooth, but take care not to over-beat or it will become runny. For the topping, mix the icing sugar with the cinnamon.

Take the sponges out of the oven and leave to cool on the tray. When cool, lift them off with a fish slice. Sandwich them together with the vanilla cream cheese filling and dust with the cinnamon icing sugar.

LOW-GLUTEN BLUEBERRY SPELT WHOOPIE

+ Makes 8 whoopies (7–9cm across) + Prep 20 minutes + Cook 8 minutes

When I was little we used to drive to Poland for our holidays. I remember crossing the Polish border, where children would wait to swap baskets of freshly picked blueberries with us for packets of chewing-gum. I would sit in the back of the car with a basket to myself. Blueberries are rich in vitamins A, C and E and beta-carotene, and of all the fresh fruit and vegetables, they provide the highest amount of health-protecting antioxidants, which help prevent cancer.

When I was asked to develop some spelt recipes by a lovely Italian café in Notting Hill, I thought of this combination. Not only do you benefit from low gluten with the spelt, but you also have the health benefits of the fantastic blueberry. It works really well for breakfast instead of a muffin.

Preheat the oven to 200°C/400°F/gas 6 and line a baking tray with grease-proof paper. Sieve the spelt flour and bicarbonate of soda into a bowl and stir in the sugar.

Mix the buttermilk with the melted butter and beaten egg.

Fold the wet ingredients into the dry ingredients with a large metal spoon – use the 'figure of eight' action – keeping air in the mix until you have an even colour (do not over-mix). Stir in the blueberries. Pipe or spoon 16 x 4cm dollops (at least 4cm high) on to the baking tray, spacing them well apart to allow for spreading, and bake in the preheated oven for 8 minutes.

While the sponges are cooking, you can start to make the filling. Cream the butter and icing sugar together and add the cream cheese and vanilla. Mix until the filling is smooth, but take care not to over-beat or it will become runny. Stir in a little blueberry juice if you like.

Take the sponges out of the oven and leave to cool on the tray. When cool, lift them off with a fish slice and sandwich them together with the vanilla cream cheese filling. I think these look lovely with the tops just dusted with icing sugar.

SPONGE

180g spelt flour

1 level teaspoon bicarbonate of soda

115g caster sugar

110g buttermilk

60g melted butter

1 free-range egg (50g), beaten

100g frozen or fresh blueberries

FILLING

50g very soft butter

100g icing sugar, sifted

150g Philadelphia cream cheese

1 teaspoon good-quality vanilla extract or essence

a little blueberry juice (optional)

TOPPING

50g icing sugar, sifted

LOW-GLUTEN WHITE CHOCOLATE AND CRANBERRY SPELT WHOOPIE

+ Makes 10 whoopies (4–5cm across) + Prep 20 minutes + Cook 8 minutes

Cranberries and white chocolate work really well together in this, a development on my blueberry spelt whoopie. Cranberries are one of nature's superfoods and are valued for their ability to prevent urinary tract infections. They benefit from being high in antioxidants, support the health of the cardiovascular system and may help reduce the risk of cancer. Their flavour can be quite sharp, so I have matched them with white chocolate in this delicious little cake.

SPONGE

180g spelt flour

1 level teaspoon bicarbonate of soda

115g caster sugar

100ml buttermilk

60g melted butter

1 free-range egg (50g), beaten

100g frozen cranberries

100g white chocolate chips

FILLING

50g very soft butter

100g icing sugar, sifted

150g Philadelphia cream cheese

1 teaspoon good-quality vanilla extract or essence

a little cranberry juice (optional)

TOPPING

50g icing sugar, sifted

Preheat the oven to 200°C/400°F/gas 6 and line a baking tray with grease-proof paper. Sieve the spelt flour and bicarbonate of soda into a bowl and stir in the sugar. Mix the buttermilk with the melted butter and beaten egg.

Fold the wet ingredients into the dry ingredients with a large metal spoon – use the 'figure of eight' action – keeping air in the mix until you have an even colour (do not over-mix). Stir in the cranberries and white chocolate chips. Pipe or spoon 20 x 4cm dollops (at least 4cm high) on to the baking tray, spacing them well apart to allow for spreading, and bake in the preheated oven for 10 minutes.

While the sponges are cooking, you can start to make the filling. Cream the butter and icing sugar together and add the cream cheese and vanilla. Mix until the filling is smooth, but take care not to over-beat or it will become runny. Stir in a little cranberry juice if you like.

Take the sponges out of the oven and leave to cool on the tray. When cool, lift them off with a fish slice and sandwich them together with the vanilla cream cheese filling. I think these look lovely with the tops just dusted with icing sugar.

GLUTEN-FREE LIME DRIZZLE WHOOPIE

+ Makes 9 whoopies (7–9cm across) + Prep 20 minutes + Cook 8 minutes + Decorate 10 minutes

Limes are great for digestion, and are supposed to aid weight loss (although I'm not so sure about the weight loss benefits of lime in a whoopie!) Psychologically I think the benefits of enjoying the whoopie will be huge. This whoopie also benefits from being gluten-free. I like my lime curd quite sharp, but if you have a sweet tooth just add 20g more sugar. Use a silicone whisk to stir the curd if you can, as metal can cause it to discolour.

First, make the lime curd filling. For this you need a glass bowl that will fit over a pan. Put the lime juice, zest and sugar into the bowl, add the butter, eggs and egg yolks, and whisk together. Place the bowl over a pan of barely simmering water and stir until the lime curd is thick and blended. Set aside to cool.

Preheat the oven to 200°C/400°F/gas 6 and line a baking tray with grease-proof paper. Sieve the almonds and bicarbonate of soda together twice, from a height. Add the lime zest.

Cream the butter and sugar together in a bowl, using a hand-held electric whisk (or in a free-standing mixer using the whisk attachment), until pale. Scrape down the bowl while whisking. Once the mixture is pale, slowly add the beaten egg a little at a time while continuing to whisk. Whisk the egg whites in a bowl and fold them into the whoopie mix alternately with the dry ingredients, with a large metal spoon – use the 'figure of eight' action – keeping air in the mix until you have an even colour (do not over-mix). Pipe or spoon 18 x 4cm dollops (at least 4cm high) on to the baking tray, spacing them well apart to allow for spreading, and bake in the preheated oven for 8 minutes.

While the sponges are cooking, make the lime drizzle by mixing the lime juice with the icing sugar.

Take the sponges out of the oven and leave to cool on the tray. When cool, lift them off with a fish slice. Drizzle them with the lime drizzle mix and set aside for about 2 hours to dry. Sandwich them together with the lime curd.

SPONGE

180g ground almonds

1 level teaspoon bicarbonate of soda

zest of 2 limes

60g butter

115g caster sugar

2 free-range eggs (50g), beaten

2 free-range egg whites (50g)

For the lime drizzle

juice of 2 limes

30g icing sugar, sifted

FILLING

juice and zest of 4 limes

100g caster sugar

100g soft butter

4 free-range eggs (50g), beaten

2 free-range egg yolks (50g)

LOW-GLUTEN JASMINE, ORANGE, SPELT AND ALMOND WHOOPIE

+Makes 10 whoopies (7–9cm across) +Prep 20 minutes +Cook 8 minutes

Jasmine is a plant rich in antioxidants, which break down the free radicals in cancer-growing cells. Jasmine and orange make a great match, so I have made a low-gluten whoopie with them. Jasmine syrup is made by Monin, and you can buy it from www.creamsupplies.co.uk.

SPONGE

180g spelt flour

1 level teaspoon bicarbonate of soda

115g caster sugar

100g buttermilk

60g melted butter

1 free-range egg (50g), beaten

1 teaspoon orange blossom water

½–1 teaspoon very strong jasmine syrup

FILLING

50g very soft butter

100g icing sugar, sifted

150g Philadelphia cream cheese

1 teaspoon jasmine syrup

TOPPING

50g icing sugar, sifted

Preheat the oven to 200°C/400°F/gas 6 and line a baking tray with grease-proof paper. Sieve the flour and bicarbonate of soda into a bowl and stir in the sugar. Mix the buttermilk with the melted butter and beaten egg.

Add the wet ingredients to the dry ingredients and fold in with a large metal spoon – use the 'figure of eight' action – keeping air in the mix until you have an even colour (do not over-mix). Add the orange blossom water and jasmine syrup. Pipe or spoon 20 x 4cm dollops (at least 4cm high) on to the baking tray, spacing them well apart to allow for spreading, and bake in the preheated oven for 8 minutes.

While the sponges are cooking, you can start to make the filling. Cream the butter and icing sugar together and add the cream cheese and the jasmine syrup. Mix until the filling is smooth, but take care not to over-beat or it will become runny.

Take the sponges out of the oven and leave to cool on the tray. When cool, lift them off with a fish slice. Sandwich them together with the jasmine cream cheese filling and top with a dusting of icing sugar.

EGGLESS FRUIT WHOOPIE
+ Makes 12 whoopies (4 5cm across) + Prep 20 minutes + Cook 10 minutes

Whether you have an egg allergy, or can't eat egg for religious reasons or because you are a vegetarian, it is still lovely to have a rich fruit cake. So here is a great recipe that uses no eggs. It can be used to make a celebration whoopie – the snowman on page 213 is particularly good with this base – and decorated according to the occasion. It is the simplest whoopie to make – you just mix everything together and bake.

Put the mixed peel, sultanas, raisins, currants and lemon zest into a bowl. Add the brandy and leave to soak for an hour.

Preheat the oven to 200°C/400°F/gas 6 and line a baking tray with greaseproof paper. Sieve the flour, ginger and mixed spice into a bowl and stir in the sugar and nuts. Chop the cherries and add to the flour – a coating of flour will prevent the cherries sinking to the bottom of the whoopie. Mix the milk with the sunflower oil. Pour the apple juice into a jug. Mix the wet ingredients into the dry ingredients and add the soaked fruit. Pipe or spoon 24 x 4cm dollops (at least 4cm high) on to the baking tray, spacing them well apart to allow for spreading, and bake in the preheated oven for 8–10 minutes.

While the sponges are cooking, you can start to make the filling. Cream the butter and icing sugar together and add the cream cheese and the brandy or rum. Mix until the filling is smooth, but take care not to over-beat or it will become runny.

Take the sponges out of the oven and leave to cool on the tray. When cool, lift them off with a fish slice. Sandwich them together with the brandy or rum cream cheese filling and dust with icing sugar.

SPONGE
50g mixed peel

75g sultanas

75g raisins

75g currants

zest of 1 lemon

45ml brandy or rum

225g self-raising flour

1 level teaspoon
  ground ginger

2 level teaspoons
  mixed spice

50g soft light brown sugar

25g hazelnuts, crushed

75g stoned ripe cherries

120g milk

50ml sunflower oil

250ml apple juice

FILLING
50g very soft butter

100g icing sugar, sifted

150g Philadelphia
  cream cheese

1 teaspoon brandy or rum

TOPPING
50g icing sugar, sifted

GLUTEN-FREE VANILLA WHOOPIE
+Makes 8 whoopies (7–9cm across) +Prep 20 minutes +Cook 8 minutes

This little whoopie is both gluten-free and nut-free. You can fill it with jam and lightly whipped double cream and have yourself a gluten-free Victoria sponge, or try some vanilla cream cheese icing. It can also be used as a base for the recipes for wacky and celebration whoopies, if you want to make them for people with allergies.

SPONGE
170g soya flour

1 level teaspoon bicarbonate of soda

100g buttermilk

1 teaspoon good-quality vanilla extract or essence

80g butter

100g soft light brown sugar

70ml milk

1 free-range egg (50g), beaten

FILLING
50g very soft butter

100g icing sugar, sifted

150g Philadelphia cream cheese

1 teaspoon good-quality vanilla extract or essence

Preheat the oven to 200°C/400°F/gas 6 and line a baking tray with grease-proof paper. Sieve the soya flour and bicarbonate of soda into a bowl. Mix the buttermilk with the vanilla and set aside.

Cream the butter and sugar together in a bowl, using a hand-held electric whisk (or in a free-standing mixer using the whisk attachment), until pale. Scrape down the bowl while whisking. Once the mixture is pale, slowly add the beaten egg a little at a time while continuing to whisk. Once the egg has been incorporated, fold in the wet and dry ingredients with a large metal spoon – use the 'figure of eight' action – keeping air in the mix until you have an even colour (do not over-mix). Pipe or spoon 16 x 4cm dollops (at least 4cm high) on to the baking tray, spacing them well apart to allow for spreading, and bake in the preheated oven for 8 minutes.

While the sponges are cooking, you can start to make the filling. Cream the butter and icing sugar together and add the cream cheese and vanilla. Mix until the filling is smooth, but take care not to over-beat or it will become runny.

Take the sponges out of the oven and leave to cool on the tray. When cool, lift them off with a fish slice. Sandwich them together with the classic vanilla cream cheese filling.

GREEN TEA WHOOPIE

+ Makes 8 whoopies (4–5cm across) + Prep 2½ hours + Cook 8 minutes

There are records of green tea being drunk in China since 1191. It is extremely high in antioxidants, and it is thought that regular green tea drinkers have less risk of heart disease and of developing certain types of cancer. Green tea powder is called matcha and is used in puddings in Japan – it can take up to an hour to grind 30g of matcha. Here is a fantastic whoopie using a good-quality green tea powder, which you can buy from www.chah.co.uk. (Don't try to make this using green tea leaves, as it won't work.) It goes very well with chocolate, so I have filled this whoopie with a dark chocolate mousse.

First make the chocolate mousse for the filling. Melt the chocolate in a bowl over a saucepan of barely simmering water. While the chocolate is melting, whisk all 6 egg whites in a clean dry bowl until the soft peak stage. Mix the egg yolks with the melted chocolate and fold in the egg whites a quarter at a time. Put into the fridge and leave to set for 2 hours.

Preheat the oven to 200°C/400°F/gas 6 and line a baking tray with grease-proof paper. Sieve the flour, green tea and bicarbonate of soda into a bowl. Put the buttermilk into a jug and set aside.

Cream the butter and sugar together in a bowl, using a hand held electric whisk (or in a free-standing mixer using the whisk attachment), until pale. Scrape down the bowl while whisking. Once the mixture is pale, slowly add the beaten egg a little at a time while continuing to whisk. Once the egg has been incorporated, fold in the wet and dry ingredients with a large metal spoon – use the 'figure of eight' action – keeping air in the mix until you have an even colour (do not over-mix). Pipe or spoon 16 x 4cm dollops (at least 4cm high) on to the baking tray, spacing them well apart to allow for spreading, and bake in the preheated oven for 10 minutes.

While the sponges are cooking, mix the icing sugar with the green tea powder for the topping.

Take the sponges out of the oven and leave to cool on the tray. When cool, lift them off with a fish slice. Sandwich them together with the chocolate mousse filling, spooning it in (do not spread or the air will come out of the mousse), and top with the other half. Dust with the icing sugar.

SPONGE

200g plain flour

2 heaped teaspoons green tea powder

1 level teaspoon bicarbonate of soda

90ml buttermilk

80g butter

100g caster sugar

1 free-range egg (50g), beaten

FILLING

4 free-range eggs (50g), separated

2 extra free-range egg whites (50g)

200g dark chocolate

TOPPING

50g icing sugar, sifted

GLUTEN-FREE CHOCOLATE
AND RASPBERRY WHOOPIE

+ Makes 8 whoopies (7–9cm across) + Prep 20 minutes + Cook 7 minutes + Decorate 20 minutes

This gluten-free chocolate whoopie is made with ground almonds and sandwiched with a raspberry vanilla filling. It looks really pretty and is delicious as a pudding, whether you are gluten-intolerant or not.

SPONGE

140g ground almonds

40g cocoa powder

1 level teaspoon
   bicarbonate of soda

90ml buttermilk

1 teaspoon good-quality
   vanilla extract or essence

80g butter

140g soft light brown sugar

1 free-range egg (50g),
   beaten

2 free-range egg whites
   (50g)

FILLING

50g very soft butter

100g icing sugar, sifted

150g Philadelphia
   cream cheese

1 teaspoon good-quality
   vanilla extract or essence

100g fresh raspberries

TOPPING

140g icing sugar

2 tablespoons water

2–3mm pink food
   colour paste

Preheat the oven to 200°C/400°F/gas 6 and line a baking tray with grease-proof paper. Sieve the ground almonds, cocoa powder and bicarbonate of soda into a bowl. Mix the buttermilk with the vanilla and set aside.

Cream the butter and sugar together in a bowl, using a hand-held electric whisk (or in a free-standing mixer using the whisk attachment), until pale. Scrape down the bowl while whisking. Once the mixture is pale, slowly add the beaten egg a little at a time while continuing to whisk. Once the egg has been incorporated, fold in the wet and dry ingredients, then whisk the egg whites in a bowl and fold them into the whoopie mix with a large metal spoon – use the 'figure of eight' action – keeping air in the mix until you have an even colour (do not over-mix). Pipe or spoon 16 x 4cm dollops (at least 4cm high) on to the baking tray, spacing them well apart to allow for spreading, and bake in the preheated oven for 7 minutes.

While the sponges are cooking, you can start to make the filling. Cream the butter and icing sugar together and add the cream cheese and vanilla. Mix until the filling is smooth, but take care not to over-beat or it will become runny. Stir in the fresh raspberries.

To make the topping, put the icing sugar into a bowl and add the water, a little at a time, stirring until you have quite a thick paste but one that is loose enough to pipe or spoon on to the whoopies. Add the colour paste to three-quaters of the mixture, a little at a time, on the end of a spoon, and leave the rest for the white feather effect.

Take the sponges out of the oven and leave to cool on the tray. When cool, lift them off with a fish slice. Sandwich them together with the raspberry vanilla cream cheese filling and dust with icing sugar.

SUGAR-FREE SWEET POTATO, CARROT AND SULTANA SPELT WHOOPIE

+ Makes 10 whoopies (3–4cm across) + Prep 20 minutes + Cook 10 minutes

My boys loved orange food when they were little, so here is a whoopie to make for your toddlers if they like it too. There is no added sugar – the sweetness is gained from the sweet potato and carrot, and because I've used spelt flour they're low in gluten. Perfect for a children's birthday party.

Preheat the oven to 200°C/400°F/gas 6 and line a baking tray with grease-proof paper. Sieve the spelt flour, cinnamon and bicarbonate of soda into a bowl. Mix the sunflower oil with the honey and beaten egg and set aside.

Mix the wet ingredients into the dry ingredients with a large metal spoon – use the 'figure of eight' action – keeping air in the mix until you have an even colour (do not over mix). Stir in the grated carrot, mashed sweet potato and sultanas. The mixture will be quite stiff. Pipe or spoon 20 x 2cm dollops (at least 4cm high) on to the baking tray, spacing them well apart to allow for spreading, and bake in the preheated oven for 8–10 minutes.

Take the sponges out of the oven and leave to cool on the tray. When cool, lift them off with a fish slice and sandwich them together with fromage frais.

SPONGE

70g spelt flour

a pinch of ground cinnamon

1 level teaspoon bicarbonate of soda

1 tablespoon sunflower oil

1 teaspoon runny honey

1 free-range egg (50g), beaten

50g carrots, grated

100g sweet potatoes, dry-roasted and mashed

30g sultanas

FILLING

100g fromage frais

FEVERFEW CUPCAKE

+Makes 12 cupcakes   +Prep 15 minutes   +Cook 20 minutes   +Decorate 5 minutes

Karen, my lovely freelance baker at the Crazy Baker, has, would you believe, a flour allergy (she can eat it, but working with it and breathing it in gives her headaches and itchiness). She also gets terrible migraine headaches, so her mum grows feverfew in the garden – it's a plant whose leaves help to relieve migraine. The flowers aren't edible but the leaves can be eaten in a salad. The cakes are as light as air – refreshing and zingy – and you don't need to be a migraine sufferer to enjoy them.

SPONGE

160g self-raising flour
140g butter
160g sugar
zest of 1 lemon
2 free-range eggs (50g), beaten
50ml milk
50g feverfew leaves, chopped

TOPPING

120g icing sugar, sifted
2 tablespoons lemon juice
24 feverfew leaves

Preheat the oven to 180°C/350°F/gas 4 and put 12 paper cases into a muffin tray. Sieve the flour into a bowl.

Cream the butter, sugar and lemon zest in a bowl, using a hand-held electric whisk (or in a free-standing mixer using the whisk attachment), until pale. Scrape down the bowl while whisking. Once the mixture is pale, slowly add the beaten eggs a little at a time while continuing to whisk. Once the eggs have been incorporated, fold in the flour and milk with a large metal spoon – use the 'figure of eight' action – keeping air in the mix until you have an even colour (do not over-mix). The mixture should be of dropping consistency. Stir in the chopped feverfew leaves. Spoon the mixture into the paper cases, filling them halfway up, and bake for 15–20 minutes, checking at 12 minutes. The cupcakes should have risen and the top should feel springy. A wooden skewer stabbed into the sponge should come out clean.

While the cupcakes are cooking, mix the icing sugar and lemon juice together. The mixture should be quite loose.

When the cupcakes are ready, take them out of the oven. Drizzle the lemon icing over the top while they are still warm and finish each one with 2 feverfew leaves.

GLUTEN-FREE ORANGE ALMOND CUPCAKE

+ Makes 12 cupcakes + Prep 25 minutes + Cook 2 hours

I've been making these cakes for fashion shoots for the last ten years as they last well when left sitting around all day, and models and photographers really enjoy them. The sponge is very moist, so orangey and delicious that you would never guess it was suitable for a gluten allergy sufferer.

First, put the oranges into a pan of water and bring to the boil. Simmer for 1½ hours, until the oranges are really soft, then remove them from the water and set aside to cool.

Preheat the oven to 180°C/350°F/gas 4 and put 12 paper cases into a muffin tray.

Separate the eggs. Whisk the egg yolks and 100g of the caster sugar in a bowl for about 20 minutes, using a hand-held electric whisk (or in a free-standing mixer using the whisk attachment), until pale. Scrape down the bowl while whisking. Whisk the egg whites in a second bowl until stiff, then add 100g of the sugar and continue to whisk to make a meringue mixture.

When the oranges have cooled, cut them into quarters and remove the white pith in the centre. Whiz the oranges in a blender. Fold the orange mixture, meringue and ground almonds into the egg yolk mixture with a large metal spoon – use the 'figure of eight' action – keeping air in the mix until you have an even colour (do not over-mix).

Spoon the mixture into the paper cases, filling them halfway up, and bake for 15–20 minutes, checking at 12 minutes. The cupcakes should have risen and the top should feel springy. A wooden skewer stabbed into the sponge should come out clean.

When the cupcakes are ready, take them out of the oven and leave them to cool in the tray. Top with flaked almonds and a dusting of icing sugar.

SPONGE

2 whole oranges, including the skin

3 free-range eggs (50g), separated

200g caster sugar

200g ground almonds

TOPPING

50g toasted flaked almonds

50g icing sugar, sifted

EGG-FREE VANILLA SPONGE CUPCAKE

+Makes 12 cupcakes +Prep 15 minutes +Cook 20 minutes +Decorate 15 minutes

Karen, one of my bakers, has been baking for twenty-eight years. At her last bakery she had a lot of Indian customers, and this is an eggless cake she came up with for them. The sweetness comes from the condensed milk, and soda water is used to lighten the cake. It is an all-in-one mix and takes five minutes to put together. Use it as a sponge base for any of the recipes in the wacky and celebration chapters. For the passionfruit pulp, just spoon out the insides of some passionfruit.

SPONGE

280g plain flour

10g icing sugar

1 level teaspoon
baking powder

½ level teaspoon
bicarbonate of soda

200ml condensed milk

60g melted butter

100ml milk

1 teaspoon good-quality
vanilla extract or essence

100ml soda water

TOPPING

50g very soft butter

100g icing sugar, sifted

150g Philadelphia
cream cheese

1 teaspoon good-quality
vanilla extract or essence

100ml passionfruit pulp

Preheat the oven to 180°C/350°F/gas 4 and put 12 paper cases into a muffin tray. Sieve the flour, icing sugar, baking powder and bicarbonate of soda twice into a bowl. Mix the condensed milk with the melted butter, milk and vanilla.

Mix the wet ingredients into the dry ingredients with a large metal spoon – use the 'figure of eight' action – keeping air in the mix until you have an even colour (do not over-mix) and adding the soda water at the last moment. Spoon the mixture into the paper cases, filling them halfway up, and bake for 15–20 minutes, checking at 12 minutes. The cupcakes should have risen and the top should feel springy. A wooden skewer stabbed into the sponge should come out clean.

While the cupcakes are cooking, you can start to make the topping. Cream the butter and icing sugar together and add the cream cheese and vanilla. Stir in 50ml of the passionfruit pulp. Mix until the topping is smooth, but take care not to over-beat or it will become runny.

When the cupcakes are ready, take them out of the oven and leave them to cool in the tray. Pipe the passionfruit cream cheese topping over the top of each cupcake and drizzle with the rest of the passionfruit pulp.

EGG-FREE CHOCOLATE CUPCAKE

+ Makes 10 cupcakes + Prep 15 minutes + Cook 20 minutes + Decorate 15 minutes

My friend Sara is a fantastic baker. She gave me this recipe for a flourless cake and I thought I should definitely include it here, since it contains vinegar and bicarbonate of soda and reminds me of my first forays into baking. I have to say this recipe is a lot more successful than my attempts back then!

Preheat the oven to 180°C/350°F/gas 4 and put 10 paper cases into a muffin tray.

Sieve the flour, cocoa powder and bicarbonate of soda into a bowl and stir in the sugar and salt.

Make three wells in the flour and add the vinegar, vanilla and vegetable oil. Pour in the milk and mix quickly and thoroughly. This mixture is very runny. Spoon the mixture into the paper cases, filling them halfway up, and bake for 15–20 minutes, checking at 12 minutes. The cupcakes should have risen and the top should feel springy. A wooden skewer stabbed into the sponge should come out clean.

While the cupcakes are cooking, you can start to make the topping. Cream the butter, icing sugar and cocoa powder together and add the cream cheese. Mix until the filling is smooth, but take care not to over-beat or it will become runny.

When the cupcakes are ready, take them out of the oven and leave them to cool in the tray. Pipe the chocolate cream cheese icing over the top of each cupcake.

SPONGE

180g plain flour

30g cocoa powder

1 level teaspoon
  bicarbonate of soda

175g caster sugar

1 level teaspoon salt

1 tablespoon white wine
  vinegar or distilled vinegar

1 teaspoon good-quality
  vanilla extract or essence

90ml vegetable oil

250ml milk

TOPPING

50g very soft butter

80g icing sugar, sifted

20g cocoa powder

150g Philadelphia
  cream cheese

INDEX

ACKNOWLEDGEMENTS

I have to start by thanking my agent Clare Hulton for taking me on. Without her this fantastic journey wouldn't have happened and it has been such fun. Thank you.

Also Lindsey Evans, my editor at Penguin, for believing in the Whoopie, being so easy to work with and becoming a friend in such a short time. Thanks to Sarah Fraser and Alistair Richardson for making the shoot such fun and making the layout and pictures so beautiful. Thanks also to Annie Lee for checking and double-checking all the text.

Thank you to Brigitte Knoche, my brilliant head chef, who has worked with me tirelessly, with a smile, throughout the development of the Crazy Baker and who repeatedly tested all the recipes. Thanks also to Karen Street, our freelance baker, for her professionalism, making the recipe testing so easy and having a laugh daily.

Thanks to my great friend Jackie Michaelsen for always being at the forefront of my every career move and encouraging me along the way.

Thanks to Richard Bertinet for inspiring me to bake commercially.

Thanks also to my boys Harry, Michael and Alex for being the most dedicated food tasters and not minding if their lunatic wife/mother was working all hours as long as the dinner was on the table. Oh, and Harry, thanks for the commas!

Thanks to my parents for all their love, support and generosity.